CÉSAR FRANCK

CÉSAR FRANCK AT THE ORGAN

CÉSAR FRANCK

A TRANSLATION FROM THE
FRENCH OF VINCENT D'INDY
WITH AN INTRODUCTION BY
ROSA NEWMARCH   ✄   ✄   ✄

DOVER PUBLICATIONS, INC.
NEW YORK

Published in Canada by General Publishing Company, Ltd., 30 Lesmill Road, Don Mills, Toronto, Ontario.

Published in the United Kingdom by Constable and Company, Ltd., 10 Orange Street, London WC 2.

This Dover edition, first published in 1965, is an unabridged and unaltered republication of the work first published by John Lane, The Bodley Head, London, in 1910. The present edition is published by special arrangement with The Bodley Head, Ltd., 10 Earlham Street, Cambridge Circus, London W.C.2.

Standard Book Number: 486-21317-X

Library of Congress Catalog Card Number: 65-14031

Manufactured in the United States of America
Dover Publications, Inc.
180 Varick Street
New York, N.Y. 10014

INTRODUCTION

To most readers the charm and peculiar value of M. Vincent d'Indy's volume on César Franck will be found in the fact that it is a veritable artistic gospel ; the life and message of a great teacher told by the most intimate and devout among his disciples. Throughout the book, in a warm and vital current, runs the note of enthusiasm and personal affection ; while at the same time we are aware of a strong and just mind which guides the pen and controls the tendency to sentimentality, or exaggerate praise. M. d'Indy's conscience is too sensitive and his insight too clear to permit of his being biased in his artistic judgments. Nevertheless to those who mistrust the personal note in biography and believe that after his death a man is rarely well served by those who would serve him best, the very attractions and merits of M. d'Indy's book may seem to be also its weaknesses. For there still remains a regrettably large number of the musical public who know very little of César Franck's work, and who will hesitate to accept in its fulness of enthusiasm the pupil's verdict upon the master. It is for this reason that I undertook to furnish the English edition of M. Vincent d'Indy's book with a short introduction which keeps two aims in view : to set forth for the benefit of the uninformed, and with due respect, the unimpeachable credentials of its author, and to strengthen his position by showing how writers of widely different artistic creeds unite with him in his judgment upon César Franck the man and musician.

It would be impossible to understand the musical movement which has been progressing in France since 1870 without having first observed the remarkable ascendency which Franck's personality and teaching—ethical and artistic—have exercised upon a generation of rising composers, many of whom are now representative of all that is most genuine and noble in French musical art. M. Romain Rolland, in his " Musiciens d'aujourd'hui," shows us that the indifference to music in its higher forms which caused Berlioz to be misunderstood and neglected in his lifetime by his own compatriots was a phase through which society passed with the advent of the Second Empire. Prior to 1840, it is evident from Berlioz's own memoirs that there existed in France a certain degree of musical sensibility and appreciation. Then came the enthusiasm for Rossini, and afterwards for Meyerbeer, which degenerated into a craze for opera of a merely frivolous and meretricious kind. This was the period of trills, roulades and insincerities, of which Bizet said toward the close of the sixties : " it is utterly dead. Let us bury it without tears or regret and—go ahead." Already the tide showed signs of turning, but the public was still apathetic. It is a remarkable fact that the two principal schools of literature which existed in France during the middle of the nineteenth century, the romantic and the naturalistic, were callous, if not hostile, to music. M. Rolland instances Hugo, Dumas, the brothers de Goncourt, Théophile Gautier, Balzac and Lamartine, as having all been indifferent to the art and even contemptuous of it. It needed the calamitous events of 1870 to awaken a new artistic conscience and new tastes in France. In this connection we are reminded of a similar occurrence in the history of culture, when Russia, recovering from the strain and stress of the year 1812, gave birth to a new and consciously national school of art and literature.

The great influences which have affected the growth of music in France since 1870 are twofold. First we have the Wagnerian movement which took a great hold upon the intellectual youth of France. It was good in so far as it awoke a more general interest in the art; but those who lived much in France at the time when the Wagnerian craze was at its most acute crisis realised, even then, that, although stimulating, it was not a fertilising influence. It is not amid the crowds of devout and often intolerant pilgrims who journeyed to Bayreuth in the eighties, that we shall discern the personalities who were to carry on the best traditions of the art in France. Most of the

young generation were more or less affected by
Wagnerism ; but the sane and lasting element in
this French musical renaissance must be sought
in another direction ; amid a group of quiet
workers who frequented a modest apartment in
the Boulevard Saint-Michel and learnt their art
from the most retiring and unpretentious of teachers
—César Franck. "He stood outside the Wagnerian movement, in a serene and fecund solitude,"
writes M. Romain Rolland. "To the attraction
which he exercised by his genius, his personality, and
his moral greatness upon the little circle of friends
who knew and respected him, must be added the
authority of his scientific knowledge. In the face
of the Wagnerian art, he unconsciously resuscitated
the spirit of John Sebastian Bach, the infinitely
rich and profound spirit of the past. In this way
he found himself unintentionally the head of a school
and the greatest educational force in contemporary
French music."

Bruneau, a critic whose outlook is very different
from that of the writer whom I have just quoted,
names Franck as one of the three regenerators of
modern music. Speaking of the period of operatic
decadence to which I have already referred, when
heroes and heroines died agreeably before our eyes to
a cheerful valse rhythm and paused in moments of
tragic intensity to emit strings of *fiorituri* and shakes,
he says : "The overwhelming success of such works
almost dealt a death-blow to music. A German,

Richard Wagner; a Frenchman, Hector Berlioz; and a Belgian who wished to belong to our glorious school, and therefore asked to become naturalised—César Franck, saved the art. The first knitted up the Beethoven traditions and wedded symphony to the drama; the second, a fervent disciple of Gluck, linked his romanticism directly to classic art; the third, going back still further into the past, and taking root there, mingled the polyphonic riches of Bach with the treasures of harmony and melody which he left us. We cannot too greatly thank, admire, and venerate them."

Thus we see Franck, for so many years misunderstood and slighted by his official contemporaries, becoming surely and steadily recognised as one of the chief artistic influences of the nineteenth century. M. d'Indy's book shows us what he has done for France. Nor are there wanting signs that his influence has extended in some measure to this country, where a genius of our own, Edward Elgar, has, consciously or unconsciously, realised a similar union of traditional faith with complete artistic liberty. The performance of a representative work by César Franck has an immense concern for the student of musical history, because he has solved, more successfully perhaps than any composer of his day, the question of the enlargement and revivification of classical forms without effecting their ultimate destruction.

In the last five or six years Franck's works have

received considerable attention in this country. That great artist, Eugène Ysaye, may be said to have popularised his Sonata for violin and piano. His Symphonic Variations for piano and orchestra, and the Symphonic poem "Les Djinns," for the same combination, have been heard at many concerts in London and the provinces. His masterpiece, "The Beatitudes," has been given at Cardiff, in part at Hereford, and in its entirety in Glasgow, and more recently at the Sheffield Festival (1908), under Mr. Henry J. Wood. Some of his compositions, however, such as the delightful "Psyche," have suffered an incomprehensible neglect. From the master I pass to his pupil and biographer.

As recently as March of the present year M. Vincent d'Indy made his first public appearance in England in the dual capacity of conductor and composer.* On that occasion I wrote for the programme-book a brief account of the composer and his career, which I propose to reproduce here with greater fulness of detail.

In introducing Vincent d'Indy's personality to a London audience, I described him not only as the most illustrious of Franck's pupils, but also as the master's most devoted friend, a qualification which I believe he would prefer to all others. To this master he owes not merely the priceless advantages of inspired teaching, but the untarnished purity of the artistic and ethical ideals which he has consistently followed throughout

* March 27, 1909, at a Queen's Hall Symphony Concert.

his career. Naturally, this does not constitute M. d'Indy's sole claim to eminence. He has his own strongly-marked individuality, which is sufficient to ensure him a great place in the world ; but the influence of Franck blends so subtly with all he is and does that to ignore it would be to misunderstand the finest qualities of his work—its clearness, sincerity, and noble orderliness ; its firm workmanship, and its peculiar strength which is the outcome of faith and enthusiasm.

Vincent d'Indy was born in Paris, March 27, 1851. His family came from the picturesque mountain region of the Cévennes. Here the musician spent much time in his youth, and the familiar landscape forms the background of many of his musical works. While still a lad he studied the piano with Diémer, and theory and composition with Lavignac. Although his talents were remarkable, it was not at first intended that he should become a professional musician. It was only after submitting a pianoforte quartet to César Franck, and receiving his encouraging criticism that he resolved to study seriously. The war of 1870 proved an interruption to his work, for he took an active share in the defence of Paris ; and it was not until 1873 that he actually joined Franck's organ class at the Conservatoire. Here he won a second prize in 1874, and a *primus accessit* the following year.

On leaving the Conservatoire he became choirmaster to Colonne, and, for experience' sake, took the post of second drummer in his orchestra. During this year (1875) his overture " The Piccolomini " was produced by Pasdeloup at the Concerts Populaires, and won him recognition as a composer of high and serious aims. Afterwards he altered this work and added, first a prologue, entitled " Wallenstein's Camp " (1880), and then a third section " The Death of Wallenstein." It was this Trilogy—by many critics considered his masterpiece—that he conducted at Queen's Hall on the occasion to which I have already referred.

The principal works of the succeeding years were : the overture " Antony and Cleopatra " (1876) ; " La Forêt Enchantée " a symphonic ballad (1878) ; the pianoforte quartet Op. 7 ; an operetta " Attendez-moi sous l'orme " (1881). In 1886 he won the first prize in the competitions organised by the City of Paris with a dramatic legend " Le Chant de la Cloche," the poem written by himself on the basis of Schiller's " Lay of the Bell." The orchestral legend " Sauge-Fleurie " and the " Symphonie Cévenole " also date from about this time. His second Symphony was produced at the Concerts Lamoureux in 1904. " Fervaal," an opera in three acts and a prologue, and " L'Etranger," in one act, were both mounted for the first time in Brussels ; the former on March 12, 1897 ; the latter in January 1903.

In an article by M. Hugues Imbert (*The Musician*, November 17, 1897), the writer mentions three great influences which, he considers, have helped to

mould Vincent d'Indy's style : " Nature, Berlioz,
and Wagner." I have already spoken of an influence
which seems to me more intimate and far-reaching
than that of Berlioz or Wagner ; but undoubtedly in a
considerable number of the composer's works a keen
feeling for nature is a predominant quality.

Speaking of the many-sidedness of this gifted personality, M. Romain Rolland says : " There are no
shadows within him. His thought and his art are as
clear as his glance, which gives such youthfulness to
his physiognomy. He feels it a necessity to judge,
order, classify and unify. There is no mind more
completely French than his. . . . This need of clarity
is the ruling principle of his artistic temperament.
And this is the more remarkable because his nature
is far from being simple. By the mere fact of his
wide musical education, and constant desire to
learn, it is enriched by a number and variety of
elements which almost contradict one another. We
must realise that M. d'Indy is one of the musicians
best acquainted with the music of the past and of
foreign nations ; musical forms of all times and
all lands float through his thoughts and he is not
quite decided upon any of them. . . . We must
also bear in mind that he has come in contact,
direct or indirect, with all the greatest musical
personalities of our time, Wagner, Liszt, Brahms and
César Franck, and has willingly submitted to their
attraction ; for he is not one of those egotistical
geniuses who carry the thought of their own interests

into everything ; those great omnivorous spirits who see nothing, seek nothing, enjoy nothing save with the idea of assimilating forces which may prove useful to themselves. He abandons himself freely, happy in rendering homage to others and submitting himself to their charm. Somewhere he speaks of 'the irresistible need of transformation' which exists in all artists. In order not to be submerged by this wealth of elements and opposing influences, it is needful to have a great force of passion or of will which can eliminate, select and transform them. M. d'Indy eliminates very little : he organises. He employs in his music the qualities of a commander : intelligence of aim and patient will-power to attain, a complete knowledge of the means at his disposal, a sense of order and a mastery of himself and his work. In spite of the variety of materials which he employs the *ensemble* is always clear."

If this eclecticism, and this power of assimilation and reorganisation, detract somewhat from the individuality of an artist's creative work, they at least fit him in the highest degree to be a critic and an educator. This is a side of M. d'Indy's activity which cannot be ignored in any Introduction which pretends to throw light upon this book and its author. I will, therefore, complete my prefatory remarks with a short reference to that great work, the outcome of his faith and devotion, which exists as a living and glorious monument to the memory of César Franck.

The *Schola Cantorum* was founded in the first

instance by M. Vincent d'Indy in conjunction with M. Charles Bordes, director of the Chanteurs de Saint-Gervais, and the well-known organist M. A. Guilmant. In the earlier prospectuses issued by its founders the aims of the institution were limited to formulating a reformation of the church music by means of a return to the great models of the past. The Gregorian system was to be accepted as the enduring basis of the church music, with the addition of Palestrina and other music which conformed to these schools. But this ideal, when carried into practice, although it had the laudable result of restoring much of the old ecclesiastical music, was found to be too restricted a foundation on which to build a new art. "The spirit of inquiry and the feeling for modern life gradually got the better of these principles," says M. Romain Rolland.* From Gregorian music and the school of Palestrina, examples of which were sung by the Chanteurs de Saint-Gervais in Holy Week under the direction of M. C. Bordes, they passed on to the works of Heinrich Schütz and the Italian and German composers of the seventeenth century, and then to the masterpieces of Bach, Rameau and Gluck. From the modest origins of the *Schola Cantorum* was evolved the idea of a school of music which should answer to modern requirements. The prime mover in this enlargement of ideals was M. Vincent d'Indy, and when in 1900 he became head of the *Schola* he moved

* "Musiciens d'aujourd'hui." Hachette, Paris, 1908.

into more spacious quarters, found in an old-world house in the Rue Saint-Jacques, where he proceeded to carry out his cherished plan. What these wider ideals were we may gather from his inaugural address, delivered on November 2, 1900.

" Art is a microcosm," he said, " which passes like the world itself through successive periods of youth, maturity and age ; which never perishes, but continually renews itself. It is not a closed circle, but a spiral, perpetually ascending and progressing. I intend to make my pupils follow the same movement as the art itself, so that having gone through the transformations to which music has been subjected in the course of centuries, they may emerge from their period of study better equipped for the conflict of these modern days, because they will have lived, so to speak, the life of their art, and will have assimilated in their natural order the forms which have succeeded each other logically through the various periods in the development of the art."

The whole object of this method of historical teaching was the refreshment of modern music at the well-spring of tradition. In the decorative art of plain song and the architectural art of Palestrina, the founder of the *Schola Cantorum* believed that the student of to-day could find innumerable suggestions for fresh rhythmic, melodic and harmonic devices. Here was the true nourishment for our modern dryness of spirit. Founded in a spirit of sane eclecticism, and vitalised by an immense and enthusiastic

faith in classic tradition—interpreted in the spirit
rather than the letter—the *Schola Cantorum* has
flourished and gained each year in *prestige*. It is a
kind of second and more modern Conservatoire.

Starting with twenty-one pupils in 1896, last year
it numbered 320. It boasts nine classes for composition, over eight of which M. d'Indy himself
presides. It is as active in giving concerts and
performances of works which are rarely heard as it
is in teaching. Branches have been formed at Lyons,
Marseilles, Bordeaux, Avignon, Montpellier, Nancy,
Epinal, Montluçon, Saint-Chamond, and Saint-Jean-
de-Luz. The *Schola Cantorum* has also its publishing
house whence have been issued a number of fine
editions of old works,* and on the modern side the
Edition Mutuelle, published by the composers themselves, who thus remain the proprietors of their
works. An indirect outcome of this movement is
the French Bach Society, founded in 1905, by
M. Gustave Bret, a former pupil of the *Schola*.

When we reckon up these numerous and far-
reaching spheres of activity and remember that they
all owe their existence to the teaching of César
Franck,† we feel that it is difficult to exaggerate

* Among the old works re-issued by this institution are the
"Orfeo" and the "Incoronazione di Poppea" of Monteverde,
edited by M. Vincent d'Indy.

† "Our venerated 'Father' Franck is to some degree the
grandfather of this *Schola Cantorum;* for it is his method of
teaching that we shall strive to continue and apply here." From
an address by M. Vincent d'Indy, November 1900.

his influence upon the musical development of France. Nor, if we came to consider the question more closely, need we perhaps restrict the area of his influence to France alone. In Belgium he has many devoted followers, and an indefatigable propagandist in the person of Eugène Ysaye. In England the scattered seed of his sowing has not fallen upon infructile soil. It is time, then, that we knew something more of this righteous spirit and poetic thinker whose place in music is not so far removed from that of Bach and Beethoven. No monumental biography of César Franck has yet been given to the world. Perhaps the simplicity and uneventfulness of his life, which left him little time for travel or correspondence, will save him from the doubtful glory of being commemorated in a colossal "Life and Letters," wherein all the small indignities of his humanity might be mercilessly exposed to view. Up to the present moment this tender and sincere tribute from the pupil to the master remains the most complete and authoritative record of Franck's personality and career. The translation, although it is from the language I heard most frequently from my mother in childhood into one with which the habit of later years has made me still more familiar, is doubtless far from perfect. But it has been undertaken in something of the same spirit of enthusiastic veneration which inspires the original, and I can only hope I have not done too great an injustice to a book the success of which in England and America I have very much at heart.

P.S.—Scarcely were the final proofs of the foregoing Introduction in the hands of the printers when
I received from Paris a copy of M. Camille Mauclair's latest musical essays : " La Religion de la
Musique." * Turning over the fascinating pages in
which so many aspects of the art are treated with
such delicate perception and from a standpoint all
too rare—from that of the worshipper of Music
rather than of Musicians—I came upon the chapters
entitled " Deux Impressions sur César Franck."
Here, I felt was an appreciation which had a special
value ; which would crown and complete the varied
array of judgments which I had already cited in the
earlier pages of my Introduction. For M. Mauclair's
impressions are neither those of a contemporary composer, nor of a scientific musician. Their significance
and peculiar interest lie in the fact of their being
wholly unprofessional—if I may use the term in this
connection. They are the ideas of man less occupied
with the realisation than with the love of music ; who
regards it as the latest religion revealed to modern
scepticism. He, too, believes that Franck's mission was
to save the art in that moment of prostration which
followed upon " the monstrous Wagnerian irrup-
tion," the close of which threatened to destroy all
musical initiative, leaving room only for the alter-
natives of timid imitation, or a hesitating return to
the formulas of the past. It was amid the general
disorganisation which succeeded the death of

* La Religion de la Musique, par Camille Mauclair. Paris,
1909. Librairie Fischbacher.

Wagner that César Franck appeared "like the faithful shepherd who restores confidence and order to his terror-stricken flock when the storm is spent. Unknown or misunderstood, he was yet able, by the charm and faith of his gentle genius, to check on a dangerous down-grade the young men who, a few years later, were to form the sole cohesive group of the French school." He showed the young and enthusiastic generation that music should be loved for itself rather than for the sake of the audacious personality who had moulded it to his will. He showed them, too, the futility of trying to follow Wagner along a dramatic path that he alone could tread. "He recalled Gluck, Rameau, Bach, and Beethoven and his persuasive teaching saved modern music."

César Franck alone could speak with authority and make this new, circumflecting course a possibility. "Any other musician (at that time)," says M. Mauclair, "would have advised an anti-Wagnerian reaction. The question, however, was not to avoid imitating Wagner by doing the opposite to what he did ; but to retrace once more after the general upheaval, the natural relations between music and all those things which the human soul will always crave to express. . . ."

"The Wagnerian vortex avoided ; the theatre neglected for a sufficient time to allow the echo of Bayreuth to die away and certain manifestations of the French spirit to reappear on the French stage

('L'Etranger,' 'Pelléas,' 'Louise'); symphony and sonata restored to an honourable position; researches undertaken into musical origins; musical criticism revived; the liberal teaching of the *Schola*, a direct emanation from the spirit of Franck—here we see the results of the peaceable, serious and loving intervention of that retiring old man who, free from prudery, lived like a saint."

Passing on from the man to his music, M. Mauçlair enumerates *Psyché*, the *Symphony*, the *Quintet*, the *Violin and Pianoforte Sonata*, *The Beatitudes*, portions of *Redemption* and *Hulda*, the *Organ Chorales*, the *Prelude*, *Aria and Finale*, the *Chorale Prelude and Fugue* for piano, as masterpieces which will never fade, and to which, since Bach and Beethoven, nothing can be compared in the domain of pure harmony. Schumann, he thinks, may have more nervous energy, Liszt and Berlioz may be greater colourists, Brahms more complex, Borodin more strange and exotic, but none of these masters is so intimately musical, none so serenely linked to the classicism of Bach. " No one else has that faculty of suave and sensuous mysticism, that unique charm, that serene plenitude of fervour, that purity of soaring melody, above all, that power of joy which springs from a religious effusion, that radiant whiteness resulting from a harmony at once ingenuous and ecstatic. There is no severity in this evangelical mysticism. Undoubtedly the *Organ Chorales* and pianoforte works are of powerful construction and

have the magnificent rectitude which proceeds
directly from Bach. But Bach is formidable; he
thunders, he has the robust faith of the Middle
Ages, his rhythm is colossal; even his gaiety is as
alarming as the laughter of a giant. Franck is
enamoured of gentleness and consolation, and his
music rolls into the soul in long waves, as on the
slack of a moonlit tide. It is tenderness itself;
divine tenderness borrowing the humble smile of
humanity."

But while doing full justice to the mild and
saintly qualities of Franck's nature, M. Mauclair
discerns also the elements of passion and romanticism, of which we become aware in such works as
the *Sonata for Violin and Piano* and the symphonic
poem *Le Chasseur Maudit*. But he considers that
Franck's ardours are invariably dominated by a
purity which will always remain the principal feature
of his inspiration. " A purity which is neither dry
nor severe, but smiling, loving and gentle, like a
Correggio seen against a decorative background by
Puvis de Chavannes."

One more quotation I cannot resist making from
these " Impressions," because, while the following
lines sum up the work which Franck did for his art,
they contain also a prophecy which has been at least
partially fulfilled. To those who have been stirred
time after time by the wordless, psychological programme of Elgar's new symphony, this quotation will
come as an echo of their own thoughts about it. For

while we may so far disagree with M. Mauclair as
to feel that all the varied directions of music
enumerated below have been desirable, and that
each one has its special value for the progress of
the art, yet we cannot doubt that the way indicated
by Franck is the one we could least afford to lose.
Therefore we may be glad and proud that it fell to
the lot of an Englishman to take the next forward
step along the path of psychological development in
symphonic music.

"Franck," says M. Mauclair, "forms the natural
link between classicism and the polyphony to come.
The direct line of descent in pure music had been
broken by the descriptive romanticism of Liszt and
Berlioz, and finally by Wagner, whose deviations were
marvellous, but dangerous to the destinies of their
art. The intervention of Franck which was at once
traditional and innovating, set the wandering feet of
a whole generation on the right track, with rare tact
and without any reaction. This is what caused this
mystic, this visionary of the golden age of music, to
be not only the last master of the nineteenth century,
but also the one man who could assure the free evolution of the music of the future ; the evolution of
music itself, which should be neither descriptive,
theatrical, nor picturesque, but only psychological,
moving the soul and revealing the infinite by the
very song of the lyre."

CONTENTS

THE MAN

PAGE

I. HIS LIFE 29

II. THE PHYSICAL AND SPIRITUAL MAN 62

THE ARTIST AND HIS MUSIC

I. THE GENESIS OF HIS WORKS 73

II. PREDILECTIONS AND INFLUENCES 92

III. METHODS OF WORK 97

IV. FIRST PERIOD (1841–1858) 104

V. SECOND PERIOD (1858–1872) 125

VI. THIRD PERIOD (1872–1890) 159

VII. THE QUARTET IN D MAJOR 182

VIII. THE THREE ORGAN CHORALES 198

IX. THE BEATITUDES 202

THE TEACHER AND HIS HUMAN WORK

I. "FATHER" FRANCK 233

II. THE ARTISTIC FAMILY 251

LIST OF WORKS 257

BIBLIOGRAPHY 271

ILLUSTRATIONS

César Franck at the organ of Sainte-Clotilde *Frontispiece*

To face page

The Basilica Church of Sainte-Clotilde 138

César Franck with Eug. Ysaye and other musicians, on the occasion of his last concert, Tournai, April 22, 1890 170

The Monument to César Franck, by Alfred Lenoir 234

25

THE MAN

I

HIS LIFE

On December 10, 1822, the very day upon which the giant of symphony, Ludwig van Beethoven, put the finishing touches to the manuscript of a work which he justly regarded as his most perfect master-piece—the sublime Mass in D minor—a child was born into the world destined to become the true successor of the Master of Bonn, both in the sphere of sacred music and in that of symphony.

It was at Liège, in the Walloon district, that César Franck was born and spent the first years of his life, in a land which is peculiarly French, not only in sentiment and language, but also in its external aspect. What other spot recalls more nearly the central plains of France than these irregular valleys, with their abrupt lines; these waste-lands where in spring the flowering broom stretches far and wide to an almost boundless, golden horizon; these low hills on which the French traveller is astonished to recognise the same pines and beeches that clothe the cold mountains of the Cévennes? This is the land, so

Gallic in its outward appearance, so German in its customs and surroundings, which was inevitably destined to give birth to the creator of a symphonic art that was exceedingly French in its spirit of balance and precision, while at the same time it rested upon the solid basis of Beethoven's art, itself the outcome of still earlier musical traditions.

The Francks claim descent from a family of Walloon painters bearing the same name,* whose works show not only the qualities we associate with the so-called primitive painters, but also many characteristics which foreshadow the art of Rembrandt. The musician's eldest son, M. Georges César Franck, possesses a small picture, painted on copper, by one of these artists, representing the mocking of the Saviour, which in composition, if not in colouring, is interesting from this point of view. Possibly it was to a reversion to type that César Franck owed his talent for drawing, which he cultivated in his youth, and for which he retained his taste as he grew older. We shall come upon traces of it as we continue to study his life and work.

The young man's mind was directed towards

---

* The earliest of these painters was Jérome Franck, born 1540 at Herrenthal, died 1610 in Paris, whither he had emigrated, like his musical descendant, and obtained the appointment of painter to Henri III. His masterpiece is said to have been a Nativity, which he painted for the church of Les Cordeliers, destroyed during the Revolution.

music quite early in life. His father, a man of
stern and autocratic character, although engaged in
banking, had many friends in the artistic world, and
decided that both his sons should become professional
musicians.

There was no alternative but to bow to this premature decision, which, generally speaking, would be
calculated to arouse a child's disgust, or even his
active dislike of the work undertaken *invito corde*;
but fortunately in the case of César Franck the seed
of music, sown so early, fell upon a wonderfully
fruitful soil.

He had barely reached his eleventh year when,
accompanied by his father, he made a tour in
Belgium, during which he met a young artist, a year
or two older than himself, who was also touring as a
virtuoso. This child was Pauline Garcia, afterwards
known as the famous singer Madame Pauline
Viardot.

At twelve years of age he had completed his
studies at the music school at Liège, and his father,
ambitious of his success on a larger scale, emigrated
with both his sons to Paris in 1836. The father of
the future composer of *The Beatitudes* asked per-
mission to enter him at the Conservatoire. It was
not until the following year, 1837, that César was
entered as a pupil, joining Leborne's class for composition and studying the pianoforte under Zimmer-

mann. At the close of the same year he won a *proxime accessit* for fugue, but the competition for pianoforte in 1838 gave rise to a singular incident which is worth relating.

After having played the work selected—Hummel's A minor concerto—in excellent style, young Franck took it into his head, when it came to the sight-reading test, to transpose the piece which was put before him to the third below, playing it off without the least slip or hesitation.

Such exploits were not within the rules of the competition, and this audacity on the part of a pupil of fifteen and a half so shocked old Cherubini, then Director of the Conservatoire, that he stoutly declined to award a first prize to the lad, although he deserved it. But in spite of his red-tapism and dictatorial methods, the composer of " Lodoïska " was not really unjust, and proposed to the jury to recommend the audacious pianist for a special reward, outside all competition, and known by the high-sounding title of " Grand Prix d'Honneur." This is the only time, to my knowledge, that such a prize has been given at any instrumental competition in the Paris Con-servatoire.

In 1839 Franck won his second prize for fugue. The feeling for combination, so essential to this queer and useless logogriph called a " class fugue," came so naturally to the young Walloon—as to his ancestors in the days of vocal counterpoint—that he only spent a small part of the time allotted by the examiners on the completion of his work. Seeing him return home while the other students had still some hours' work before them, his father reproached him bitterly for not bestowing more care upon this test, on which his future depended. " I think it is all right," answered the lad, with a smile. All the trustful candour of César Franck, as we knew him, is already revealed in this reply.

The following year, in spite of rather an ungrateful subject set by Cherubini, he was unanimously awarded the first prize for fugue (July 19, 1840).

In 1841 he again surprised the examiners. César, as a pupil of Benoist (whom he succeeded in 1872), competed for the organ prize.

The tests for this examination were—and still are—four in number : the accompaniment of a plainchant chosen for the occasion, the performance of an organ piece with pedal, the improvisation of a fugue, and the improvisation of a piece in sonata form, both these improvisations being upon themes set by the examiners. Franck, with his wonderful instinct for counterpoint, observed that the subject given for the fugue lent itself to combination with that of the free composition, and treated them simultaneously, in such a way that one set off the other.

He tells us that he was " very successful in combining the two subjects," but the developments which grew out of this unusual method of treating the free composition ran to such unaccustomed lengths that the examiners (Cherubini was absent through illness), bewildered by such a technical feat, awarded nothing to this tiresome person. It was not until Benoist, the master of this too ingenious pupil, had explained the situation that they went back upon their first decision and decided to give the young man a *second* prize for organ! From this moment Franck became suspect in the eyes of these officials.

There remained but one great prize to stir his ambitions—the Prix de Rome. He began to prepare for the competition of the Institute. It is possible that the authorities did not *believe* he was a Frenchman,* but in any case a peremptory order from his father compelled him to leave the Conservatoire for good in the middle of the academic year.

On April 22, 1842, Franck's name was removed from the lists of our national school of music; he was admonished to follow the career of a virtuoso.

To this period belong most of his compositions for pianoforte alone : transcriptions, pieces for four hands, caprices, showy fantasias—in a word, all that

* M. Georges C. Franck reserves to himself the task of proving this on some future occasion.

then constituted the necessary stock-in-trade of the *pianist composer.*

Happily our generation no longer knows these meteoric musicians ; " comets of a season," startling all the capitals of Europe in their dazzling course, firing the fancies and feelings of the fair sex and melting bullion into current coin as they ran their romantic career.

Such were Liszt and Thalberg, to mention only the most famous.

Franck's father had dreamt of a similar existence for his eldest son, and although it was by no means suited to his taste and temperament he forced him to make the most of his talents as a pianist and to compose from time to time a certain number of pieces to play in public.

In spite, however, of this enforced labour, Franck, being a true and worthy artist, could not help seeking for new forms, even in his most insignificant pro-ductions. He did not, of course, attain to the lofty æsthetic forms which characterised his later works, but he employed novel methods of fingering, devices hitherto unused, and harmonic effects which lent a new sonority to the pianoforte. Therefore some of his early works for piano, such as the *Eclogue*, Op. 3 (1848), and the *Ballade*, Op. 9, contain innovations which may still attract the musician, especially the pianist.

The first three *Trios* (called Op. 1) also date from this time. Franck composed them while he was still at the Conservatoire, and his father dictated the dedication: *To His Majesty Leopold I., King of the Belgians.*

If I remember rightly a conversation which I once had with my master on the subject of these *Trios*, a royal audience, at which the young musician was to present his works personally to the king, was made the pretext for withdrawing him suddenly from the Conservatoire. His father based the wildest hopes upon this dedication—hopes which, alas! were not justified in the end.

I shall return to these *Trios* in the second part of this volume, especially to the first, in F♯ minor, which marks a new stage in the history of music.

No details are forthcoming respecting the two years spent by Franck in Belgium after his hasty departure from the Conservatoire. Most probably his father did not find the move as advantageous as he expected, for in 1844 we find the whole family back in Paris, installed in an apartment in the Rue La Bruyère, and with few other resources than those earned by the two sons, Joseph and César, by private lessons and concert engagements.

From this time began that life of regular and unceasing industry lasting nearly half a century, without break or pause, during which the musician's sole diversion was a concert—at rare intervals—at which one of his own works was given.

On January 4, 1846, in the concert-room of the Conservatoire (which a more liberal management than that which now reigns used to put at the disposal of *living* artists), the first performance of his Biblical eclogue *Ruth* took place. He had begun to compose the work immediately after his return to Paris. If *Ruth* won the sympathy and attention of a few musicians—sincere or not, as the case may be *— it is certain that the majority of the critics saw nothing in it but a "poor imitation" of "Le Désert," by Félicien David, who had made a sensational success two years earlier, and was still enjoying his ephemeral renown. A year or two later all the critics made use of Wagner's works when they wished to crush a new composition by unkind comparisons ; and this continued until quite recently, when the same critics adopted the singular course of exalting *a priori* every new work, regardless of its worth, and generally to the detriment of the old masterpieces. Such are the strange vicissitudes of criticism.

One of these critics in 1846, more lenient than the rest, wrote as follows : "M. César Franck is exceedingly naïve, and this simplicity, we must

* M. Georges C. Franck possesses some curious letters from celebrated composers dealing with this subject.

confess, has served him well in the composition of his Biblical oratorio *Ruth*." Twenty-five years later, September 24, 1871, a second performance of *Ruth* was given at the Cirque des Champs Elysées, and the same critic, moved to enthusiasm, and oblivious, perhaps, of the fact that he had already heard the oratorio, wrote : " It is a revelation ! This score, which recalls by its charm and melodic simplicity Méhul's ' Joseph,' but with more tenderness and modern feeling, can most certainly be described as a masterpiece."

Hard times were in store for the Franck family. The rich amateurs who formed the young men's chief *clientèle* almost all left Paris, alarmed by the political outlook, and with them vanished the pecuniary resources of the Francks.

César chose this moment to marry.

For some time past he had been in love with a young actress, the daughter of a well-known tragedian, Madame Desmousseaux, and he did not hesitate to marry her in spite of bad times and the recriminations of his parents, scandalised by his bringing *a theatrical person* into the family.

The marriage took place at the church of Notre-Dame de Lorette, where César Franck was then organist, on February 22, 1848, in the very midst of the Revolution. To reach the church the wedding-party had to climb a barricade, and the bride and bridegroom were willingly helped in this delicate operation by the insurgents who were massed behind this improvised fortification.

Very shortly after his marriage, Franck, having lost all his pupils, and being misunderstood by his father, whom he could no longer supply with funds, found it necessary to leave his parents and make an independent home of his own. He was now compelled to work twice as hard as before, in order to replace by quantity the quality of the lessons he had lost, and to undertake many inferior tasks. But, his time being henceforward at his own disposal, he resolved at all costs to reserve an hour or two daily for composition, or the study of such musical and literary works as would be elevating to his mind—"time for thought," as he himself used to say.

To the last days of his life nothing was allowed to interfere with his resolution. We owe to it all his great works.

In 1851 Franck made his first attempt at a dramatic work : an opera, as it was called in those days. He did not return to this form of composition until near the end of his career.

For his first effort he chose a Dutch subject, the action of which takes place towards the close of the seventeenth century. Alphonse Royer and Gustave Vaes, fashionable librettists of the day, supplied him with a book which was neither better nor worse than those in use at that period. Full of enthusiasm, the musician set to work, and gave himself no rest until he had finished the first three acts of his *Valet de Ferme* (" The Farmer's Man "), as the opera was entitled. As he found it impossible to give up his teaching and daily occupations, even for an hour, he devoted the greater part of his nights to composition, and worked so hard that the opera, begun in December 1851, was finished and orchestrated early in 1853. Poor Franck paid dearly for this overwork ; for he fell into such a state of nervous prostration that, for a time, he not only lost all power of composing, but could not even think, every mental effort leaving him utterly exhausted.

And, after all, it was time wasted from a practical point of view, for when a few years later Alphonse Royer became Director of the Opera—which must have seemed to Franck a most unlooked-for piece of luck—he absolutely declined to mount *Le Valet de Ferme*, on the specious pretext that, being himself the author of the libretto, the regulations of the Opera forbade him to do so. It may be said with truth that he had already been well paid out of the scanty emoluments of the poor composer who had almost ruined his health over the work.

Towards the close of his career the master did not greatly value this hastily written score. " It is not

worth printing," he used to say to those who spoke
of it to him.*

In the meanwhile the Abbé Dorel, a worthy
priest who, as curate of Notre-Dame de Lorette, had
upheld the young organist in his first trials, and had
taken an active part in his marriage, was appointed
to the parish of Saint-Jean-Saint François au Marais,
a church which had just been presented with a fine
organ by Cavaillé-Coll, the gifted inventor, who died
young. The worthy Abbé lost no time in appoint-
ing his young friend at Notre-Dame de Lorette to
the post of organist, and Franck, delighted to find
himself in possession of such a splendid instrument,
declared that his organ " was an orchestra ! "

It was not, however, until some years later that
he found that quiet and fixed haven which—I
have no hesitation in affirming—was the starting-
point of a new phase of his art, and from which dates
what may be described as his second musical period.
The existing basilica of Sainte-Clotilde had just been
completed, replacing the modest church of Sainte-
Valère, and Cavaillé-Coll, then at the zenith of his
genius as a poet-craftsman, had just constructed his
masterpiece for it, that wonderful instrument that
even now—after fifty years' use—has kept all its
freshness of *timbre* and fulness of tone.†

* Information received from M. Georges C. Franck.
† " If you only knew how I love this instrument," " Father "

It was a very different affair from the modest *orchestra* of Saint-Jean-Saint-François, and so César Franck, actuated far more by artistic feeling than by the thought of gain, tried for the post of organist to Sainte-Clotilde—where he had been choir-master since 1858—and obtained it, in spite of intrigues and many rival competitors.

Here, in the dusk of this organ-loft, of which I can never think without emotion, he spent the best part of his life. Here he came every Sunday and feast-day—and towards the end of his life every Friday morning too—fanning the fire of his genius by pouring out his spirit in wonderful improvisations which were often far more lofty in thought than many skilfully elaborated compositions; and here, too, he assuredly foresaw and conceived the sublime melodies which afterwards formed the groundwork of *The Beatitudes.*

Ah! we know it well, we who were his pupils, the way up to that thrice-blessed organ-loft—a way as steep and difficult as that which the Gospel tells us leads to Paradise. First, having climbed the dark, spiral staircase, lit by an occasional loophole, we came suddenly face to face with a kind of ante-diluvian monster, a complicated bony structure,

Franck used to say to the Curé of Sainte-Clotilde; "it is so supple beneath my fingers and so obedient to all my thoughts!" Quoted from an address delivered by Canon Gardey, October 22, 1904.

breathing heavily and irregularly, which on closer examination proved to be the vital portion of the organ, worked by a vigorous pair of bellows. Next we had to descend a few narrow steps in pitch-darkness, a fatal ordeal to high hats, and the cause of many a slip to the uninitiated. Opening the narrow *janua cæli*, we found ourselves suspended as it were midway between the pavement and the vaulted roof of the church, and the next moment all was forgotten in the contemplation of that rapt profile, and the intellectual brow, from which seemed to flow without any effort a stream of inspired melody and subtle, exquisite harmonies, which lingered a moment among the pillars of the nave before they ascended and died away in the vaulted heights of the roof.

For César Franck had, or rather *was*, the genius of improvisation, and no other modern organist, not excepting the most renowned executants, would bear the most distant comparison with him in this respect.*
When, on very rare occasions, one of us was called upon to take the master's place, it was with a kind of superstitious terror that we ventured to let our profane fingers caress this supernatural thing, which was accustomed to vibrate, to sing, and to lament

---

* I recollect a certain offertory based upon the initial theme of Beethoven's seventh Quartet which nearly equalled in beauty the work of the Bonn master himself. Those who heard this improvisation will certainly not contradict my opinion.

at the will of the superior genius of whom it had become almost an integral part.

Sometimes the master would invite other people, friends, amateurs, or foreign musicians, to visit him in the organ-loft. Thus it happened that on April 3, 1866, Franz Liszt, who had been his sole listener, left the church of Sainte-Clotilde lost in amazement, and evoking the name of J. S. Bach in an inevitable comparison.

But whether he played for some chosen guest, for his pupils, or for the devout worshippers during service, Franck's improvisations were equally thoughtful and careful, for he did not play in order to be heard, but to do his best for God and his conscience' sake. And *his best* was a sane, noble, and sublime art.

To describe these improvisations, the true value of which we only realised when there was no chance of hearing them again, would be an impossible task ; I must leave to those who, like myself, were habitual guests at these musical feasts the delight of a memory which will vanish all too soon, even as these inspired and ephemeral creations have already passed away.

Thus for ten years Franck lived the quiet and retiring life of an organist and teacher, and the feverish creative activity of his youth was succeeded by a period of calm, during which he composed nothing but organ pieces and church music. But

this calm was only the precursor of a new and
decisive development, which was to enrich musical
art with many a sublime masterpiece.

All through his life Franck had desired to write
a musical work on that beautiful chapter of the
Gospels, *The Sermon on the Mount*. He had already
made several attempts (which I shall consider in the
critical part of this work) on this subject which was
so well suited to his devout mind and strong, ardent
temperament. In 1869 he was at last able to set to
work upon a poem, which may fall short as regards
poetry and versification, but at least shows respect
for the scriptural text; while paraphrasing it in
such a way as to allow of many fine musical
developments.

No sooner was he in possession of this literary
basis, than he threw himself into the task with such
energy that he composed the first two parts without
a break.

This work was interrupted by an event to which
no Frenchman could remain indifferent—the Franco-
Prussian War of 1870. Although born in Belgium,
Franck was French in heart, and by adoption.

Too old to take active service himself, Franck saw
his young disciples dispersed by the ill-winds of our
reverses. Abandoning counterpoint, organ and piano,
for bayonet and rifle, they joined those valiant
improvised armies which, for six months, France

succeeded in mustering in opposition to the victorious invaders. Several of these young men never saw their dear master again—others, like Alexis de Castillon, succumbed when the war was at an end, worn out by the hardships of the winter campaign.

Three of them, like Franck himself, were shut up in Paris : Henri Duparc, Arthur Coquard, and myself. At that time I had not yet ventured to show the master any of my formless attempts at composition.

One evening, during an interval between mounting guard at the outposts, we went to see him in his quiet rooms in the Boulevard Saint-Michel, and found him quivering with emotion over an article in the *Figaro* which celebrated in poetic prose the virile pride of our dear Paris, wounded, but resisting to the end. " I must set it to music," he exclaimed as soon as he caught sight of us. A few days later he sang us, with febrile enthusiasm, the result of his work, which overflowed with patriotic inspiration and the ardour of youth :

I am Paris, queen of all the cities, &c.

This ode has never been published, and it was the first time that a musician had ventured to set music to a prose poem.

In 1872 a very curious event happened in the master's career : he was appointed, nobody knows how—and he himself, a stranger to all intrigue, understood it less than the rest—Professor of Organ at the Conservatoire.

Benoist, who had reached the age limit (he entered on his duties in 1822, the year which saw the foundation of the Conservatoire), retired into well-earned repose ; how did it happen that a Minister—clearsighted by some lucky chance—hit upon the organist of Sainte-Clotilde, who was so singularly unofficial in mind and manner ? The mystery has never been elucidated.

Be it as it may, César Franck took over the organ class on February 1, 1872, and became from that moment an object of animosity, conscious or unintentional, to his colleagues, who always refused to regard as *one of themselves* an artist who placed Art above all other considerations, and a musician who loved Music with a sincere and disinterested devotion.

The same year, interrupting his work on *The Beatitudes*, he wrote, almost without intermission, the first musical setting of *Redemption*, an oratorio in two parts, to a rather poor libretto by Edouard Blau, and Colonne, then at the beginning of his career as a conductor, directed the first performance at a Concert Spirituel, on Thursday in Passion Week, 1873.

The performance was far from satisfactory. Colonne had not then the experience he has since acquired, and another composer, whose oratorio of imposing dimensions was to be given on Good Friday, took up nearly all the rehearsals which should have been divided between the two concerts. Good " Father " Franck, guileless and trusting, had to be satisfied— and actually was satisfied, being the most unexacting of men—with a most perfunctory performance, which did not do the work justice in any way. So scanty were the hours of rehearsal that he had to cut out the symphonic interlude between the two sections of his work, a number which he subsequently rewrote.

With the exception of *Les Eolides*, a symphonic poem on a subject by Leconte de Lisle, which made a passing appearance in 1876 on the programme of one of the concerts at the Porte Saint-Martin, conducted by Lamoureux, and was not in the least understood by the public, Franck devoted the six years which followed the completion of *Redemption* to his oratorio *The Beatitudes*, which was only completed in 1879, and consequently occupied ten years of his life.

Conscious that he had produced a fine work, the musician, whose simple nature made him the perpetual prey of illusions in all questions of practical life, imagined that the Government of the country to which his genius did honour could not fail to take an interest in the performance of such a lofty manifestation of art, and that if the Minister once became acquainted with his work he would undoubtedly appreciate its beauty and forward its success. He therefore organised a private performance of *The Beatitudes* at his own house, after carefully inquiring what date would be likely to suit the Minister of Fine Arts, and personally invited the critics of the leading papers and the Directors of the Conservatoire and the Opera. The solos were confided to pupils of the Conservatoire, and the choruses—which are such an important part of the work—to some twenty singers, disciples of Franck, or pupils in his organ class.

Delighted at the prospect of this performance in miniature, Franck intended to preside at the piano in person, but—first disappointment of many to come— he sprained his wrist the day before, in closing a carriage door. He came at once to ask me to take his place, and, proud as I was of the honour, I was somewhat oppressed by the responsibility, for I had but one day in which to master the score so that I might play it fairly well to the select company on whose support the musician was putting implicit reliance.

All was ready, and the performers awaiting only the arrival of the guests in order to begin. At half-past eight a message arrived from the Minister to the effect that, " to his great regret, he found it impossible to be present," &c. The Directors of the Conservatoire and the Opera had already made excuses ; while as to the leading critics, they were detained that evening by something far more important than the hearing of a work of genius : it was the first night of a new operetta at one of the women's theatres.

One or two of these gentlemen of the Press did put in an appearance, but fled in a few minutes from this region, so remote from the chief Boulevards. Only two of the guests stayed to the end ; Edouard Lalo and Victorin Joncières paid Franck this mark of respect.

Franck was somewhat depressed and disenchanted by the result of this performance from which he had hoped so much. Not that he had lost faith in the beauty of his work, but because not one of us, his best friends, scrupled to tell him that a performance of *The Beatitudes* in its entirety, at any concert, seemed to us impossible ; for which we are now ready to cry *mea culpa*. In consequence of this, he made up his mind—not without some bitterness of heart—to cut up the work into sections ; and it was in this form that he offered it to the Committee of the Société des Concerts du Conservatoire, who kept him waiting a long time before they included one of the eight parts in their programmes.

Fourteen years later, Colonne, who wanted to atone for the failure of *Redemption*, gave the whole of *The Beatitudes* with all the care necessary to ensure an artistic performance. The effect was overwhelming, and henceforth the name of Franck was surrounded

by a halo of glory, destined to grow brighter as time
went on. But the master had been dead for three
years.

After the ill-fated private performance of *The
Beatitudes*, the Minister of Fine Arts, overcome,
perhaps, by remorse, attempted to get Franck
appointed to one of the classes for composition at the
Conservatoire, vacant on the retirement of Victor
Massé ; but Ernest Guiraud, composer of " Madame
Turlupin," was preferred to the creator of *The
Beatitudes*.

In consequence of this, a signal mark of favour
was bestowed upon the composer by the Government,
by way of compensation ; in company with "the
butcher, the baker, the candlestick-maker," and all
manner of "purveyors," he was raised to the high
dignity of *officer of the Academy !* Most artists were
profoundly astonished to see the purple ribbon
accorded to one who seemed worthy of the red ; the
only person to whom this refusal of justice seemed
quite natural was the master himself.

We, his pupils, were indignant, and did not
hesitate to show it. One of us went so far as to
express this feeling in Franck's presence ; but the
composer only replied in low, confidential tones :
" Be calm, be calm—*they have given me every hope for
next year.*" It was not, however, until five or six
years later that Franck received the ribbon of a

Chevalier of the Legion of Honour, several music-
asters, loafers in the Ministerial ante-rooms, having,
of course, received precedence of him. But it
would be wrong to suppose that this honour was
bestowed upon the musician, the creator of the fine
works which do honour to French art. Not in
the least ! It was to the official who had completed
over ten years service that the cross was presented,
and the decree of August 4, 1885, only says :
" Franck (César Auguste), professor of organ."
Decidedly, the French Government was not happy
in its dealings with him !

It was in consequence of this nomination, and to
show that he was something better than a *professor of
organ*, that his friends and pupils raised a subscription
to cover the expenses of a concert devoted entirely
to his compositions.

The " Franck Festival" took place on January 30,
1887, at the Cirque d'Hiver, under the bâton of
J. Pasdeloup and the composer himself. The programme was as follows :

FIRST PART
CONDUCTED BY M. JULES PASDELOUP

1. *Le Chasseur Maudit*, symphonic poem.
2. *Variations Symphoniques*, for piano and orchestra.
   M. Louis Dièmer.
3. Second Part of *Ruth*, a Biblical eclogue.
   Mlle. Gavioli, M. Auguez and Chorus.

SECOND PART

CONDUCTED BY THE COMPOSER

4. *March* and *Air de Ballet*, with chorus, from the
   unpublished opera *Hulda*.
5. *Third and Eighth Beatitudes.*
   Mmes. LESLINO, GAVIOLI, BALLEROY.
   MM. AUGUEZ, DUGAS, G. BEYLE.

The performance by an orchestra lacking in
cohesion and insufficiently rehearsed was a de-
plorable affair. Pasdeloup, courageous innovator
and first champion of symphonic music in France,
was then growing old and losing authority as a
conductor; he went entirely wrong in the *tempo* of
the finale of the *Variations Symphoniques*, which ended
in a breakdown. As to Franck, he was listening too
intently to the vibration of his own thoughts to pay
any attention to the thousand details for which a
conductor must always be on the alert. The interpretation of *The Beatitudes* suffered in consequence,
but such was his good-nature that he was the only
person who did not regret the wretched performance,
and when we poured out to him our bitter com-
plaint that his works should have been so badly
given, he answered, smiling and shaking back his
thick mane of hair : "No, no, you are really too
exacting, dear boys; for my own part, I was quite
satisfied ! "

The last years of Franck's life brought to light

four masterpieces which will always stand out clear
and luminous in the history of French music : the
Violin Sonata, composed for Eugène and Théophile
Ysaye, the *Symphony* in D minor, the *String Quartet*,
and, lastly, the three *Chorales* for organ, which were
his swan-song.

The *Symphony* was given for the first time on
February 17, 1889, by the Société des Concerts du
Conservatoire. The performance was quite against
the wish of most members of that famous orchestra,
and was only pushed through thanks to the bene-
volent obstinacy of the conductor, Jules Garcin.

The subscribers could make neither head nor tail
of it, and the musical authorities were in much the
same position. I inquired of one of them—a professor at the Conservatoire, and a kind of *factotum*
on the Committee—what he thought of the work.
" *That*, a symphony ? " he replied in contemptuous
tones. " But, my dear sir, who ever heard of
writing for the cor anglais in a symphony ? Just
mention a single symphony by Haydn or Beethoven
introducing the cor anglais ? There, well, you
see—your Franck's music may be whatever you
please, but it will certainly never be a symphony ! "
This was the attitude of the Conservatoire in the
year of grace 1889.

At another door of the concert-hall, the composer
of " Faust," escorted by a train of adulators, male

and female, fulminated a kind of papal decree to the effect that this symphony was *the affirmation of incompetence pushed to dogmatic lengths.* Gounod must be expiating these words in some musical purgatory; for, coming from an artist such as he was, they can neither have been sincere nor disinterested.

For sincerity and disinterestedness we must turn to the composer himself, when, on his return from the concert, his whole family surrounded him, asking eagerly for news. "Well, were you satisfied with the effect on the public? Was there plenty of applause?" To which "Father" Franck, thinking only of his work, replied with a beaming countenance: "Oh, it sounded well, just as I thought it would!" *

The *Violin Sonata,* which Eugène Ysaye took all over the world, was a source of mild delight to César Franck; but his greatest surprise was the unprecedented success of his *String Quartet,* at one of the concerts of the Société Nationale de Musique, which has done so much for the improvement of French taste, and of which Franck, who helped to found it in 1871, had been elected president a few years later.†

* Told by M. Georges C. Franck.

† The players who took part in this first performance were MM. L. Heymann, Gibier, Balbreck, and C. Liègeois.

At the performance of April 19, 1890, the members of the Société Nationale, who were only just becoming initiated into any novelties in form, showed unanimous and sincere enthusiasm for the work. The Salle Pleyel resounded with such applause as was rarely heard within its walls; the audience all rose to clap, and call for the composer, who, not being able to realise that a quartet could meet with such success, persisted in believing that these acclamations were intended for the performers. When, however, he reappeared on the platform, smiling, shy, and bewildered—he was so unaccustomed to the situation—he could no longer doubt the evidence of such an ovation, and the next day, filled with pride at this *first success* (in his sixty-ninth year!), he said to us quite naïvely : "There, you see, the public is beginning to understand me."

A few days later, April 27, a second triumph awaited him at Tournai, when he took part in a concert of his own works given by the Ysaye Quartet.

But these pleasant impressions were not of long duration. One evening, in the month of May of this same year (1890), on his way to his pupil, Paul Brand, he was struck in the side by the pole of an omnibus. He continued his way, but fainted on his arrival at Brand's house. When he recovered consciousness, he played the second piano in the *Varia-*

tions Symphoniques, which he was obliged to go through twice, and afterwards returned home to the Boulevard Saint-Michel completely tired out.

Careless of physical suffering, he continued to lead his usual hard-working life, renouncing only his personal pleasures. When his colleagues on the Committee of the Société Nationale invited him to preside at their dinner, after which he was to enjoy the surprise of a second private performance of his *Quartet*, he was obliged, on account of ill-health, to refuse himself the pleasure of taking part in these friendly festivities. He wrote to the Committee as follows :

"May 17, 1890.

" DEAR FRIENDS,

"I very much regret that I cannot join you to-night at the banquet which closes our year, from which I have never before been absent.

" My regret is all the keener because I am aware of the pleasure in store for me—the second performance of my Quartet, which was so admirably played on April 19.

" A thousand thanks for all the kindnesses and charming attentions you invariably show me, and believe in my unchanging devotion to our dear Society,

" CÉSAR FRANCK."

Towards the autumn, however, he was forced to

take to his bed on account of a very serious attack of pleurisy, and complications, due to his accident which had not been properly treated, having set in, he died on November 8, 1890.

Shortly before his death he wished to drag himself once more to his organ at Sainte-Clotilde in order to write down the proper combination of stops for the three beautiful *Chorales* that—like J. S. Bach a hundred and thirty years earlier—he left as a glorious musical testament.

The *Chorales*, the last prayer of this sincere believer, were lying on his death-bed when the priest of the basilica which had so often echoed to his serene improvisations came, at his express desire, to bring him the last consolations of the Church.

His funeral was as modest as his life had been. By special authorisation the service was celebrated in Sainte-Clotilde instead of the parish church of Sainte-Jacques, and Monseigneur Gardey preached a touching funeral sermon ; after which, without pomp or display, the procession took its way to the cemetery of Montrouge, where the earthly remains of the Master were interred in a retired corner. A few years later they were exhumed and taken to the cemetery of Montparnasse.

No official deputation from the Ministry or the Department of Fine Arts accompanied the body of César Franck to its last resting-place. Even the

Conservatoire, which reckoned him among its professors, neglected to send a representative to the
funeral of this organist whose lofty views of Art
had always seemed dangerous to the peace of this
official institution. The Director, Ambroise Thomas,
who had all his life been given to pouring forth platitudes on less worthy tombs, quickly took to his bed
when he heard that a member of Franck's family
had come to invite him to the funeral. Other important professors followed suit, and were con-
veniently taken ill in order to avoid compromising
themselves.*

Only the Master's numerous pupils, his friends,
and the musicians whom his untiring kindness had
won over to him, formed a respectful and devoted
circle around his grave. At his death César Franck
left a legacy to his country in the form of a vigorous
symphonic school, such as France had never before
produced.

Very just were the words with which Emmanuel
Chabrier, who only survived Franck a few years,
ended his touching funeral oration, delivered at the
grave in the name of the Société Nationale de
Musique :

" Farewell, Master, and take our thanks, for you
have done well. In you, we salute one of the

* The pall-bearers were Dr. Ferréot, the Master's cousin, Saint-
Saëns, Delibes and H. Dallier, who represented his organ pupils.

greatest artists of the century, and also the incomparable teacher whose wonderful work has produced a whole generation of forceful musicians, believers, and thinkers, armed at all points for hard-fought and prolonged conflicts. We salute, also, the upright and just man, so humane, so distinguished, whose counsels were sure, as his words were kind. Farewell! . . ."

Fourteen years—almost to the day—after this intimate and affectionate leave-taking, the same disciples, friends, and musicians, their number somewhat depleted, alas! by death, assembled once more in the square opposite the basilica of Sainte-Clotilde at the inauguration of the monument raised to the memory of their beloved Master. But this time they were joined by an enthusiastic crowd. With the exception of one member of the Institute, whose inexplicable jealousy pursued Franck even beyond the grave, the leading officials had shown a desire to be prominent in the places of honour ; the Director of the Beaux-Arts, and the head of the Conservatoire himself, delivered addresses which were much commented upon.

What had taken place during these fourteen years ? Quietly, and almost unobserved, the name of César Franck—once held in reverence by a few who believed in him—had now become famous.

This Administration, this Conservatoire that had

ignored, even if they had not misunderstood, this obscure organ-teacher during his life, now hastened to assert their claim to him. Numbers of composers who would have considered themselves compromised had they asked his advice in earlier days now discovered, as if by magic, that they had once been his pupils.

The Institute, however, could not be represented officially at the inaugural ceremony, because, although it had welcomed to its venerable bosom such flagrant nonentities as the composer of " Les Noces de Jeannette" or " Le Voyage en Chine "— to mention only the dead—it had never opened its doors to one of the greatest musicians who ever did honour to our native land.

But what do these transient titles and distinctions matter to those who, like Veuillot in literature, Puvis de Chavannes in painting, and César Franck in music, have earned by the beauty and sincerity of their work the right to be known as creative artists !

II

THE PHYSICAL AND SPIRITUAL MAN

PHYSICALLY Franck was short, with a fine forehead and a vivacious and honest expression, although his eyes were almost concealed under his bushy eyebrows; his nose was rather large, and his chin receded below a wide and extraordinarily expressive mouth. His face was round, and thick grey side-whiskers added to its width. Such was the outward appearance of the man we honoured and loved for twenty years; and—except for the increasing whiteness of his hair—he never altered till the day of his death. There was nothing in his appearance to reveal the conventional artistic type according to romance, or the legends of Montmartre. Any one who happened to meet this man in the street, invariably in a hurry, invariably absent-minded and making grimaces, running rather than walking, dressed in an overcoat a size too large and trousers a size too short for him, would never have suspected the transformation that took place when, seated at the piano, he explained or commented upon some fine composition, or, with one hand to his forehead and the other poised above his stops, prepared the organ for one of his great improvisations. Then he seemed to be surrounded by music as by a halo, and it was only at such moments that we were struck by the conscious will-power of mouth and chin, and the almost complete identity of the fine forehead with that of the creator of the Ninth Symphony. Then, indeed, we felt subjugated—almost awed—by the palpable presence of the genius that shone in the countenance of the highest-minded and noblest musician that the nineteenth century has produced in France.*

The moral quality which struck us most in Franck was his great capacity for work. Winter and summer he was up at half-past five. The first two morning hours were generally devoted to composition—"working for himself," as he called it. About half-past seven, after a frugal breakfast, he started to give lessons all over the capital, for to the end of his days this great man was obliged to devote most of his time to teaching the piano to amateurs, and even to take the music classes in various colleges and boarding-schools. All day long he went about on foot or by omnibus, from Auteuil to l'Ile Saint-

* M. Georges C. Franck possesses a portrait of his father by Mme. Jeanne Rongier which is undoubtedly the best and most faithful picture of the Master.

Louis, from Vaugirard to the Faubourg Poissonnière, and returned to his quiet abode on the Boulevard Saint-Michel in time for an evening meal. Although tired out with the day's work, he still managed to find a few minutes to orchestrate or copy his scores, except when he devoted his evening to the pupils who studied organ and composition with him, on which occasions he would generously pour upon them his most precious and disinterested advice.

In these two early hours of the morning—which were often curtailed—and in the few weeks he snatched during the vacation at the Conservatoire, Franck's finest works were conceived, planned, and written.

As I have already remarked, the musical work which was his everyday occupation did not prevent him from taking an interest in all manifestations of art, and more especially of literature. During the holidays spent in the little house that he rented for the summer at Quincy, he set aside a certain time for reading books, both old and new, and sometimes very serious works. Once when he was reading in the garden with that close attention he gave to all his pursuits, one of his sons, seeing him smiling frequently, inquired what he was reading that amused him so much. " Kant's 'Critique of Pure Reason,' " answered his father; " it really is very amusing." Do not these words from the lips of this musician, who was both a believer and a Frenchman, constitute one of the shrewdest judgments ever passed upon the heavy and indigestible " Critic " of the German philosopher ?

If Franck was an arduous and determined worker (during two months' holiday in 1889 he wrote the four movements of his String Quartet and mapped out the last two acts of his second opera, *Ghisèle*), his motive was neither glory, money, nor immediate success. He aimed only at expressing his thoughts and feelings by means of his art, for, above all, he was a truly modest man. He never suffered from the feverish ambition that consumes the life of so many artists in the race for worldly honour and distinction. It never occurred to him, for instance, to solicit a seat in the Institute ; not because—like a Degas or a Puvis—he disdained the honour, but because he innocently believed that he had not yet earned it.

This modesty, however, did not exclude that self-confidence which is so necessary to all creative artists, provided it is founded on a sound judgment and is free from vanity. In the autumn, when the classes were resumed and the master, his face lit up with a broad smile, used to say to us, " I have been working well these holidays ; I hope you will all be pleased," we knew for certain that some masterpiece would soon blossom forth. On these occasions the great joy of his busy life was to keep an hour or two in the evening in which to assemble his favourite pupils round the piano while he played to them the work he had just finished, singing the vocal parts in a voice which was as warm as it was grotesque in quality. He did not even scorn to ask his pupils' advice on the new work, or, better still, to act upon it, if the observations they ventured to make seemed to him really well founded.

Untiring assiduity in work, modesty, a fine artistic conscientiousness—these were the salient features in Franck's character. But he had yet another quality—a rare one—namely, goodness : a goodness that was serene and indulgent.

The word most often used by the master was the verb " to love." " I love it," he would say of a work, or even of a detail which appealed to his sympathies ; and in truth his own works are all inspired by love, and by the power of love and his high-minded charity he reigned over his disciples, over his friends, and over all the musicians of his day who had any nobility of mind ; and it is out of love to him that others have tried to continue his own good work.

We must not, however, infer from this that the master's temperament was cold and placid—far from it ; his was a fervent nature, as all his works undoubtedly bear witness.

Who among us can fail to recall his holy indignation against bad music, his explosions of wrath when our awkward fingers went astray on the organ in some ugly harmonic combination, and his impatient gesture when the bell at the altar cut short the exposition of some promising offertory? But such displays of irritability on the part of "a Southerner from the North" were chiefly directed to artistic principles, very rarely to human beings. Never during the long years I spent in his society did I hear it said that he had consciously given a moment's pain to any one. How, indeed, could such a thing have happened to him whose heart was incapable of harbouring an evil thought? He would never believe in the mean jealousy that his talent excited among his colleagues, not excluding those of some reputation, and to the day of his death he was always kindly in his judgments upon the works of others.

In an essay published in 1890 M. Arthur Coquard relates a very typical anecdote bearing on this subject.

"With what perfect sincerity," writes M. Coquard, "he enjoyed all that is beautiful in contemporary art! With what simplicity he did justice to his more fortunate fellow workers! Living composers had no juster or kinder judge than Franck —whether they bore the name of Gounod, Saint-Saëns cr Léo Delibes. Some of his last words to

me concerned M. Saint-Saëns, and I am glad to
repeat them exactly.

" It was on the Monday evening, four days before
his death. He was feeling a little better, and I
brought news from the *Théâtre Lyrique* * which greatly
interested him. Naturally, I told him all about the
first night of the season, and how ' Samson et Dalila '
had obtained a great success, and I spoke *en passant*
of my admiration for M. Saint-Saëns's masterpiece. I
can see him still, turning his worn and suffering face
towards me, and saying eagerly and almost joyfully
in that deep and vibrant tone so familiar to all his
friends : ' Very fine ! very fine ! ' "

Yes, in truth, the creator of *The Beatitudes* passed
through life his eyes fixed on a lofty ideal, without
the will, or even the power, to suspect the inherent
meanness of human nature, from which the artistic
brotherhood is, unhappily, far from being exempt.

This untiring force and inexhaustible kindness
were drawn from the well-spring of his faith ; for
Franck was an ardent believer. With him, as with
all the really great men, faith in his art was blent
with faith in God, the source of all art.

Some short-sighted writers, who are perhaps
entirely lacking in the critical sense, have tried to
compare Franck's ideal of Jesus Christ, so divinely

---

* One of the many "Lyric" theatres started in Paris since
1870, all of which had a very brief existence.

loving and merciful, with that ambiguous philanthropist whom Ernest Renan has presented to us under this name. These people can never have grasped any of the meaning of *The Beatitudes*, and would assuredly never have written such nonsense had they been privileged, like some of us, to frequent the organ gallery at Sainte-Clotilde and to witness every Sunday the act of faith so simply fulfilled by the master when, at the moment of the Consecration, interrupting the improvisation he had begun, he would leave the organ-bench, and, kneeling in a corner of the gallery, prostrate himself in fervent adoration before the Almighty Presence at the altar.

Franck was undoubtedly a believer, like Palestrina, Bach, or Beethoven before him ; confident in a life to come, he would not lower his art for the sake of fame in this one ; he had the ingenuous sincerity of genius. Therefore, while the ephemeral renown of many artists who only regarded their work as a means of acquiring fortune or success begins already to fall into the shadow of oblivion, never again to emerge, the seraphic personality of " Father " Franck, who worked for Art alone, soars higher and higher into the light towards which, without faltering or compromise, he aspired throughout his whole life.

THE ARTIST AND HIS MUSIC

I

THE GENESIS OF HIS WORKS

THOSE who wish to judge an artist's work syntheti-
cally and sincerely must begin by turning back to its
first causes—often very remote—and by trying to
trace the sources of its origin.

Whatever our views may be as to the greater or
less importance of what we agree to call artistic
personality, it is an undeniable truth, as laid down by
the rough-and-ready good sense of Bridoison, that
"One is always the son of somebody." Neither man
nor a work of art is the outcome of spontaneous
generation ; they are invariably linked to some pre-
established order, often, as I have already said, quite
remote, of which they remain the direct emanation
even at the most diverse epochs.

The evolution of Art might therefore be justly
compared with a tree whose invisible roots draw
nourishment from the fluids of the earth, which are
the sources of its material life, just as the religions of
the past form those of the artistic life. Soon the
rhythm of the tree becomes apparent ; it forces a way

through the nourishing crust of earth and emerges into the open air, rather as a passive result than as an active cause. In the same way the first craftsman of genius, profiting unconsciously by the work which has been accomplished by hidden forces, begins to reveal himself in works which are rather the incorporation of doctrine than actual forms of beauty.

From this stem, so fragile at first, which we may call Art, branches are gradually put forth, which, in their turn, engender a fresh set, and in the same way the various forms of expression in art may be said to come into existence. Every branch that is firmly grafted upon the parent stem will bring forth leaves, flowers, and fruit by the help of the fecundating sap ; but every branch which from accident, disease, or unwillingness to receive into itself the nourishing moisture becomes separated from the organic whole is inevitably destined to wither and perish.

Such branches the Gospels tell us will be cut down and cast into the fire.

The life of Art resembles that of the tree ; every creative artist, like every branch, has a mission to fulfil—namely, to contribute to the growth of the parent-stem from which he sprang. He may, of course, grow as he pleases in the direction best adapted to his nature ; his fruits may be infinitely varied ; but while he is ever pushing upward, he must not cease to draw nourishment from the traditional source. Such are the imprescriptible laws of true progress.

Because it sought its sustenance at the long-dried well-spring of pagan art, the Renaissance, although moving in leaps and bounds, and in spite of glorious and inspired efforts, never succeeded in producing anything but a sterile form of art which had no real æsthetic value.

Franck was the exact opposite of a disciple of the Renaissance. Far from regarding form as an end in itself, as did most of the painters and architects of that period, thus creating a *conventional* type of beauty injurious to the normal development of the art—still more remote from the system of certain modern " renaissants " who tend to do away with all forms because they are incapable of creating them efficiently— Franck never considered that manifestation of a work which we call *form* as anything but the *corporeal* part of the entity of an art work (" l'être œuvre d'art "), destined to serve as the visible outer covering of the *idea*, which he called " the soul of the music." We shall see, in fact, how in his works the *form* is modified according to the nature of the *idea*, while still remaining firmly based upon those great foundations which constitute the natural tradition of all art.

Although Franck owed nothing to the Renaissance, he had, on the other hand, much greater affinity, through his qualities of clearness, luminosity, and vitality, with the great Italian painters of the fourteenth and fifteenth centuries. His ancestors were Gaddi, Bartolo Fredi, and Lippi rather than the artists of the later periods. Even Perugino's angels, with their somewhat affected attitudes, have already scarcely anything in common with the angels of *Redemption*; and if we may re-discover the Virgin of *The Beatitudes* in some fresco by Sano di Pietro, it would never enter into our heads to invoke Franck's presentment of her while looking at La Fornarina, who served Sanzio for model, or even at some cleverly grouped *Pietà* by Van Dyck, or Rubens.

Franck's art, then, like that of the primitive Sienese and Umbrian painters, was an art of clear truth and luminous serenity. His light was entirely spiritual, excluding the least touch of violent colour ; for although Franck was an " expressive " artist, he was never a colourist in the true sense of the word ; we must acknowledge this defect in him ; and in this respect, again, it is impossible to associate him with the Dutch or Flemish schools.

But continuing our researches into the question of his atavic links, we shall discover another line of artists to whom he is closely related—those modest and admirable craftsmen to whom we owe the wonderful typical beauty and eurythmy of our French cathedrals. As will be seen from the picture which I have endeavoured to draw of Franck's moral nature, he shares not only the modesty, simplicity, and self-abnegation of our gentle "imagers" and builders of the thirteenth century, but also their absolute sincerity of inspiration and naïve conscientiousness in the execution of a work.

I run no risk of contradiction in asserting that no modern musician was more single-hearted and sincere, both in his work and in his life, than César Franck. None possessed in a higher degree the *artistic conscience* which is the touchstone of genius.

We may find the proof of this assertion in several of the master's compositions. In truth, an artist who is really worthy of the name can only express well that which he has himself experienced, and finds it extremely difficult to use his art as a medium for the expression of feelings which are foreign to his nature. It is remarkable that, by reason of his incapacity to suspect evil, Franck never succeeded in depicting human perversity with any success. Whenever he was compelled to deal with such feelings as hatred or injustice—in short, with *evil*—these situations are undoubtedly the weakest parts in his works. It is only necessary to look at the chorus of the Rebellious Spirits, the Unjust and the Tyrants in the fifth and seventh *Beatitudes*, to be convinced of this ; not to speak of the greater part of the role of Satan in the latter number, in which the Prince of Evil takes on the pompous and theatrical air of some demon in a picture by Cornelius or Wiertz.

It is natural, therefore, that, besides the absolute music in which he excelled, Franck—whose gifts were bound to conform to the great sincerity of his character—should have been attracted by scenes from the Bible and the Gospels, such as *The Angel and the Child, The Procession, The Virgin at the Cradle, Ruth, Rebecca, Redemption, The Beatitudes,* in which radiant hosts of angels, such as might have been dreamt of by Filippo Lippi or Giovanni da Fiesole, join with all the Just in proclaiming the infinite perfection of the Most High.

His work, like that of our poets in stone, the builders of the French cathedrals, is all a splendid harmony and a mystic purity. Even when he is dealing with secular subjects Franck cannot get away from this angelic conception. Thus one of his works is particularly interesting in this respect; I mean *Psyche*, in which he aimed at making a musical paraphrase of the antique myth.

This score is divided, as we know, into choral sections, in which the voices play the part of the classic *historicus*, relating and commenting upon the fable; and into orchestral sections, little symphonic poems meant to depict the actual drama which takes place between the two acting characters.

Let us take the principal number in the work, the

"love duet" we might call it, between Psyche and
Eros. It would be difficult to regard it otherwise
than as an ethereal dialogue between *the soul*, as the
mystical author of "The Imitation of Christ" conceived it, and a seraph sent from heaven to instruct
it in the eternal verities. This, at least, has always
been my own impression of this fascinating musical
picture.

Other composers called upon to illustrate the
same subject would not have refrained from trying
to depict love either in its physiological and most
realistic aspects (as in "Le Rouet d'Omphale,"* for
instance), or that kind of discreet and quasi-religious
eroticism which was quite the fashion a few years
ago ("Eve" and "Marie-Magdeleine" †).

I think Franck chose the better part ; and I will
even venture to affirm that in acting thus, almost
with *naïveté*, he came nearer to the true meaning of
the old myth which has had so many reincarnations
in mediæval and even modern poetry, including
"Lohengrin."

But it is particularly as regards the inspired feeling
for architecture that the comparison between Franck
and our French artists of the thirteenth century
impresses us most clearly : the judicious choice of
the first elements, infallible judgment as regards the

---

* Symphonic poem by Saint-Saëns.
† Two sacred cantatas by Massenet.

value and quality of the materials to be used, and, finally, a wonderfully balanced perception of the way to build up these materials, and of the logical sequence in which they should be presented in order to secure the perfect harmony and solidity of a musical edifice.

If, therefore, by his purity and luminousness of invention, César Franck may be linked with the primitive Italians of the beautiful period which preceded the sixteenth century, and if his Walloon descent may be considered to account for the ease with which he grasped combinations which will seem very complex to other minds, he still remains eminently French by the sense of order, style, and balance which prevail in all his works.

And perhaps this is the reason—for I prefer not to set it down to prejudice, or the misconception of what is art on their part—that the Germans do not yet understand his music, the logical clearness of which is not easily assimilated by minds, profound enough, I am willing to own, but lacking the sense of balanced proportion and good style; the incongruous Greek Walhalla near Ratisbonne, the abstruse canvases of Boecklin, and the over-lengthy symphonic poems of Richard Strauss are flagrant cases in point.

Among the art critics who have written more or less intelligently about Franck, no one has better understood and expressed the exceedingly French side of his artistic temperament than M. Gustave Derepas, Professor of Philosophy, who, in 1897, published a very accurate study of the life, the works, and the teaching of the composer of *Redemption*. I should be to blame were I not to quote some passages from this pamphlet, which is probably no longer to be found, although as far as intimate knowledge of Franck's mind is concerned, it is far more valuable than many more pretentiously written articles emanating from " authorised " critics.

In the course of a comparison between the Wagnerian conception of art and Franck's own views M. Derepas says : " César Franck's mysticism is the direct expression of the soul, and leaves him his full consciousness in his aspirations towards the divine. The human being remains intact amid the accents of love, joy, or grief. This is because the God of César Franck has been revealed to him by the Gospel, and is as different from Wotan in the ' Nibelungen ' as midday from the pallid twilight. Franck leaves to the Germans their nebulous dreams ; he clings to that part of the French temperament which, perhaps, we do not value sufficiently : good sense, clear reason, and moral equilibrium."

Later on he adds : " The atmosphere in which Franck moves is illuminated by a very clear light, and animated by a breath which is really that of life.

His music makes us neither beast nor angel. Keeping a steady balance, as far removed from materialistic coarseness as from the hallucinations of a doubtful mysticism, it accepts humanity with all its positive joys and sorrows, and uplifts it, without dizziness, to peace and serenity, by revealing the sense of the divine. Thus it tends to contemplation rather than to ecstasy. The hearer who abandons himself with docility to its beneficent influence, will recover from the superficial agitation at *the centre of the soul*, and, with all that is best within himself, will return to the attraction of the *supremely desirable* which is at the same time the *supremely intelligible*. Without ceasing to be human he will find himself nearer to God. This music, which is truly as much *the sister of prayer as of poetry*, does not weaken or enervate us, but rather *restores to the soul, now led back to its first source, the grateful waters of emotion, of light, of impulse ; it leads back to heaven and to the city of rest.*" * In a word, it leads us from egoism to love, by the methods of the true Christian mystics : from the world to the soul, from the soul to God (*ab exterioribus ad interiora, ab interioribus ad superiora*).

To love, to leave self behind in order to rise above it—this is actually the method of which we have

---

* *César Franck, étude sur sa vie, son enseignement, son œuvre*, par Gustave Derepas, docteur ès lettres, agrégé de philosophie. Paris, Fischbacher, 1897.

been speaking, and practised instinctively by the
noblest geniuses ; it was Franck's method, and gives
the clue to the secret of his style.

Let us now leave these generalisations and these
questions of artistic atavism, and endeavour to apply
the preceding remarks to the composer's works
themselves ; in the course of a synthetic analysis of
his productions we shall not fail to be struck by the
profound classicism which emanates from them.   M.
Paul Dukas, who wields a sure and graceful pen,
contributed a worthy appreciation of the master's
style, written with the most complete accuracy of
observation.   He says : "Franck's classicism is not
purely that of form ; it is not a mere filling in, more
or less sterile, of scholastic outlines, such as resulted
by the hundred from the imitation of Beethoven, and
later of Mendelssohn, and continue to grow every
year out of respect for useless traditions.   Franck's
music, it is true, seems to follow by preference the
regular designs consecrated by the genius of the
classical masters, but it is not from the reproduction
of the forms of the sonata or the symphony that it
derives its beauty.   These great musical structures,
which are in keeping with the kind of idea that needs
for its full expression the vast spaciousness and
ample periods that such large forms can offer, build
themselves up in a suitable manner under the stress
of impulse necessary to the development of the idea.

With Franck this idea is classical; that is to say, as general as possible, therefore it naturally adopts a classical form; but for this reason only, and not on account of a preconceived theory, or a reactionary dogmatism that would subordinate the thought to the form.

"Works of this kind, like bodies in which the function creates the organ, are as widely different from the schematism of most of the neo-classicists as a living organism from an anatomical model. They are as firmly cohesive on account of their hidden principle as the works in which the form is not engendered by the thought are disconnected and weak. The former will flourish and endure, while the latter will languish and pass away."

To this I would add on my own account that it is precisely because Franck continually draws upon *tradition*, instead of remaining the slave of *convention*, that his ideas have acquired the power to be absolutely original, and have put forth a sane and vigorous branch from the tree of tradition, thus bringing his personal contribution to the progress of music.

Beethoven, the noble outcome of classic force, who began by writing purely formal symphonic works, before he won the place of a genius in the upward progress of his art, marked out by the works of his third period (1815–1827) a new road, and although he himself did not travel far along it, he left it open for such of his successors as were endowed with a sufficiently robust temperament to force their way along it, knowing also how to avoid the dangers they might encounter.

The question involved no less than the transformation, or rather the renovation, of the sonata-form, that admirable basis of all symphonic art which had been accepted by all musicians from the seventeenth century onward by virtue of its harmonious logic.   Beethoven indicated the manner of this renovation, somewhat unconsciously perhaps, but not the less surely, by associating with the architectural plan of the sonata two other forms which had, so far, been essentially divided from it.

One, namely, the *fugue*, had enjoyed, with J. S. Bach and his predecessors and contemporaries, a moment of ineffable splendour ; the other, the great *variation-form*—which, let me say at once, has nothing in common with the " theme and variations " ("thème varié") which was the joy of Haydn's audiences and the despair of pianists of the romantic school—had already been anticipated by that universal spirit, J. S. Bach, and in a few very rare instances by some other composers.

These two forms, traditional perhaps, but from which the vitality appeared to be gradually ebbing away, were employed by Beethoven to revivify the languishing form of the sonata, and this was the point of departure of a new system of musical structure, which was, however, solidly based upon classical tradition.

As this is not the place in which to give a history of Beethoven's music, I will merely give as examples of this transformation the pianoforte sonatas Opp. 106 and 110, and the quartets Opp. 127, 131, and 132. Those among my readers who have carefully studied these works, which were ahead of their time, will understand my meaning.

Having cleared and lit up the way by these colossal beacons, Beethoven died ; and, strange to say, at that moment not a single individual in the three artistic nations appeared to have observed these lights. Italy, the pride of music in the sixteenth century, was then in a condition of meretricious degeneracy, from which even now she has by no means rallied. France, caught in the toils of the Judaic school of opera, was producing nothing in the sphere of symphonic music, for the quintets " of all work " of Onslow are not more worthy in this sense than Gounod's quartets, Halévy's overtures, or Meyerbeer's marches. As to Berlioz, passionate admirer of Beethoven as he shows himself in his writings—did he really understand him ? This is a matter which still needs elucidation. At any rate, he remained as remote from him as possible in his art ; and it would be difficult to find two artists more completely at the opposite poles of creative thought than the creator of the " Symphonie Fantastique " or " La Damnation de Faust " and the mind which planned the " Missa Solemnis " and the Twelfth Quartet.

As to Germany, she had in no way profited by Beethoven's indications; not a single composer attempted to take over this heritage, bequeathed, like the legendary sword of the Northern sagas, to the worthiest.

Neither Mendelssohn's elegant symphonies nor those of Spohr contributed any new elements to the old form ; Schubert and Schumann, so spontaneous, so truly original in the sphere of song or small instrumental pieces, are considerably hampered in the sonata or the symphony,—perhaps because they knew too little of the things about which Spohr and Mendelssohn knew too much ; Brahms, himself, in spite of a sense of development which may be compared, without exaggeration, to that of Beethoven, did not understand how to benefit by the valuable lessons left by the latter for future generations, and his weighty symphonic baggage must be regarded as a continuation rather than a progress.

The thread of Beethoven's discourse, broken by fate, lay unused until a young man of nineteen conceived the idea of trying to knot it up to his own ideas and to make it a solid link between new musical forms and expressions.

It was towards the close of 1841, fourteen years after the death of Beethoven, that César Franck of Liège wrote his first *Trio* (in F sharp).

How this young pupil of the Paris Conservatoire came to conceive the idea of constructing an important work upon the basis of a single theme, concurrent with other melodies which also reappear in the course of the work, thus creating a *musical cycle*—a form which Liszt alone foresaw without ever arriving at a perfect development of it—this, indeed, is and will probably always remain a mystery.

In any case, this first *Trio*, with its two generative themes, treated either fugally or in the form of the variation, as Beethoven meant it to be, was actually the point of departure of that entire synthetic school of symphony which sprang up in France late in the nineteenth century; and, for this reason, it marks an event in the history of music.

In the work of Franck himself, the *Sonata*, the *Quintet*, the sublime *Quartet*, the *Chorales*, and *The Beatitudes* are all the result of the assimilation of Beethoven's heritage by a truly creative mind.

Hence the blend of tradition and classicism in the construction and synthetic style of his works, and, as the result of this, complete freedom in the expression of his individuality, which he felt to be so firmly stayed by tradition that he could leave himself a free hand in the matter of melodic progression and harmonic aggregations; and it is with perfect justice that in the article already quoted M. Paul Dukas goes on to say : " César Franck's language is strictly individual, of an accent and quality hitherto unused, and recognisable among all other idioms. No musician would hesitate as to the authorship of one of his phrases, even if it were unknown to him. The character of his harmony and his melodic line distinguish his style from that of other musicians as clearly as with Wagner and Chopin. Perhaps it is only permissible for one endowed with such powerful musical originality to have recourse to the breadth of expression, the note, impersonal by its generality, which is the characteristic of classical art. In any case we need not fear to be mistaken in saying that it is to the union of this kind of expression, manifested in traditional forms, with a vocabulary and syntax hitherto unknown, that César Franck's music owes all its greatness."

To understand the truth of this observation it is necessary to analyse the master's style more closely, and this analysis, as we shall see, will prove that in the generality of his works the sense of what is novel and first-hand—the sense of individuality—is simply due to his conscientious application of his intimate artistic thoughts, so clear, so definite and sincere, to

the three primordial elements of musical expression :
melody, harmony, and rhythm. What, indeed, are
the principal characteristics of Franck's style but the
following qualities :

The nobility and expressive value of his melodic
phrase ;

The originality of his harmonic combinations ;

The solid eurythmy of his musical structure ?

Our master is a melodist in the highest meaning
of the word. His themes have nothing in common
with what the frequenters of the Italian Opera during
the greater part of the nineteenth century erroneously
termed *melody ;* nor do they resemble the short-winded
successions of notes which in certain modern scores
are labelled *motives.* Franck's themes are true melodies,
amply constructed upon a serious and solid basis ; he
sought them without haste, and almost always found
them in the end. In his music everything sings
continuously. He could no more conceive a piece
of music that had not a carefully chosen but very
definite melodic outline, than Ingres could have
thought of a picture apart from unimpeachable
drawing.

Equally to the richness and abundance of his
melodic vein Franck's harmony owes all its originality.
If we consider music horizontally, following the
fruitful principles of the mediæval contrapuntists,
rather than vertically according to the custom of

composers who are only harmonists, we shall find that the outlines of the various melodic phrases which are superimposed form, in this kind of music, particular combinations of notes which constitute a far stronger and more attractive style than the commonplace and incoherent sequences of chords ranged in order by music-makers who look no higher than their treatises on harmony.

But it is chiefly in the sphere of rhythm, taken in its widest sense, or, if my readers prefer it, in the sphere of musical architecture, that Franck has made himself a place quite apart from other composers. Taking up the art of construction precisely where Beethoven left it, he created what we now call the *cyclic style*—a discovery as important to symphonic music as the Wagnerian procedures were to opera— and founded on the tradition of the great classics of the past a new method of musical construction of which I shall presently give some striking examples.

In addition to this, the chief preoccupation of his whole life was to find in every divergence of musical radiation new forms—I had almost said waves—while keeping as his basis of investigation the sure and immovable principles laid down by the gathered traditions of the great musical geniuses.

II

PREDILECTIONS AND INFLUENCES

BEFORE I enter upon a special study of Franck's work as a whole, I should like to say a few words about what I may call his musical affections, as well as about his methods of working, if it can really be asserted that he consciously raised his habits to the level of a method.

The first of Franck's predilections, I might almost say his first love in music—and here we have proof of that racial atavism already alluded to—was for the works of the French musicians of the close of the eighteenth century ; Monsigny, for whose opera "Le Déserteur," a little master-piece of graceful expression, he had an unbounded admiration ; Dalayrac, from whose operas he took some of the themes of his early pianoforte pieces ; * Grétry, certain pages of whose music he could not re-read, even in his maturity, without being sincerely affected ; Méhul, by whose "Joseph" he was completely carried away. "How can I describe

* Two fantasias for piano on *Gulistan* (see list of works).

his joy and enthusiasm," writes M. Arthur Coquard,[*] " when one day he accidentally came upon the admirable duet descriptive of jealousy from 'Euphrosine and Coradin'? He sang it through several times, enraptured, and I can still see him getting up from the piano and saying with quick emotion : ' This is dramatic music—and music into the bargain!'"

Indeed, during the long period of nearly twenty years which covered the first phase of his talent it is no uncommon thing in his melodic inspiration to come upon a suggestion of the composer of "Stratonice." Certain themes in the first and fourth Trios, that of the Ballade in B major for piano, many pages in Ruth, and even in later works, might pass for motives from Méhul, if there was not already apparent a faintly discernible but unmistakably personal savour which afterwards became the typical aroma of Franck's melody. Such was the hint of future suffering which now and then crops up in the Mozartian melody of Beethoven's earliest works.

It was only in his second stage of development that Franck began to assimilate and originalise (if I may be forgiven for coining the word) this melodic style taken from his beloved French masters, which, under the influence of Bach, Beethoven, and

* César Franck, by A. Coquard, a pamphlet which appeared in 1890 and was reissued in 1904 in the Monde Musical.

Gluck, ended by becoming—from the early organ
pieces to *The Beatitudes*—that inspired and personal
melody, mentioned in the foregoing pages, which no
thoughtful musician could possibly mistake for that
of any other composer.

Continuing the list of Franck's predilections, I
must relate how certain great works signified for him
the incarnation of absolute beauty, and how he would
sometimes become so absorbed in them as to forget
all possible contingencies. Henri Duparc recollects
some pianoforte lessons at the Collège de Vaugirard
which were entirely taken up by the master's enthusiastic reading of an act from " Iphigénie en Tauride,"
organ works by Bach, and certain passages from
Weber's " Euryanthe."

When the time had flown by, the poor professor
was overcome with remorse for having spent the
lesson in these diversions instead of exercising his
pupils' fingers by copious streams of scales and
suitable studies. Yet how far more valuable to these
budding intelligences must have been these *lessons on
works !*

Besides Méhul, Gluck, Bach, and Beethoven, the
perpetual objects of his admiration, the master was
very fond of certain composers of intimate melody,
such as Schumann, and particularly Schubert, whose
Lieder were a constant source of fresh delight to him ;
he had a somewhat inexplicable affection for some of

Cherubini's works, and also for the "Préludes et Chants" of Ch. Valentin Alkan, whom he regarded as a " poet of the pianoforte."

As to the particular melodic influences which are reflected in Franck's music, is there any useful object to be gained by seeking them out and defining them ?

When I have pointed out certain melodic outlines which occasionally resemble those of J. S. Bach—not so very surprising, considering his cult for the art of the great Cantor—such as the chief theme of the fourth *Beatitude*:

when I have brought out the curious coincidence, from an æsthetic point of view, of the likeness between the initial subject of the *Symphony*:

and even that of the third *Beatitude*:

to the mysterious interrogation at the end of Beethoven's Quartet, Op. 135:

Muss es sein?

when, again, I have called attention to the Meyer-
beerian cut of certain—inferior—passages in *The
Beatitudes*, as, for example :

and the few traces of Wagnerian influence to be
found in the chromaticism of *Les Eolides*, or the use,
probably quite unconscious, of the " bell theme "
from " Parsifal " * (there was a time, I remember,
when he studied Wagner ardently, although he
cannot really be counted among the Wagnerians of
his day) ;—when I have shown all these examples, can
it be said that I have explained my master's style
any better than by my preceding observations ?   I
think not ; moreover, I do not believe that we ought
to attach very great importance to melodic resem-
blances.   The great contrapuntists and polyphonic
masters of the fifteenth and sixteenth centuries lost
nothing of their originality because—and how often
does it not occur ?—they treated the same themes.

* In the *Prélude, Choral et Fugue* for pianoforte.

III

METHODS OF WORK

In the first part of this book I have already spoken of the master's regular habits when engaged upon creative work, and of his assiduous use of the comparatively few hours which his life as a teacher permitted him to devote to composition. I want now to say something as to the manner in which he profited by these precious hours, during the twenty years or so that I had occasion to observe him.

Without going too deeply into technical details, it seems indispensable at this point to remind—or inform—my readers that the creation of any work of art, plastic or phonetic, demands, if the artist is really anxious to express his thoughts sincerely, three distinct periods of work : *the conception, the planning out, and the execution.*

The first, which we have described as the period of conception, is subdivided into two operations : the *synthetic* and the *analytic conception.* That signifies for the symphonist the laying down of the broad

lines, the general plan of the work, and the deter-
mination of its constituent elements—the themes, or
musical ideas, which will become the essential points
of this plan.

These two undertakings generally succeed each
other, but are nevertheless connected, and may
modify each other in this sense, that the nature of
the *idea* (the personal element) may lead the creative
artist to change the order of his preconceived plan ;
while, on the other hand, the nature of the *plan* (the
element of generality) may invoke certain types or
musical ideas to the exclusion of others. But
whether it be synthetic or analytic, the *conception* is
always independent of time, place, or surroundings—
I had almost added of the artist's will; he must, in
fact, wait until the materials from which his work
will be built—materials which will account for the
form while they are also influenced by it—present
themselves to his mind in a completely satisfactory
way.

This mysterious period of conception is sometimes
of long duration, especially with the great composers
(look at Beethoven's sketch-books), for their artistic
consciences compel them to exercise extreme severity
in the choice of their utterances, whereas it is the
characteristic of second-rate musicians, or those who
are infatuated with their own merits, to be satisfied
with the first matter which comes to hand, although

its inferior quality can only build up a fragile and transient edifice.

The second period in the creation of a work, which we call the planning out or ordering, is that in which the artist, profiting by the elements previously conceived, definitely decides upon the disposition of his work, both as a whole and in all its minutest details.

This work, which still necessitates a certain amount of invention, is sometimes accompanied by long moments of hesitation and cruel uncertainties. It is the time at which a composer undoes one day what it has cost him so much trouble to build up the day before, but it also brings the full delight of feeling himself to be in intimate communion with the Beautiful.

Finally, when the heart and the imagination have conceived, when the intelligence has ordered, the work, comes the last stage, that of *execution*, which is mere play to a musician who knows his business thoroughly; this includes the actual writing, the instrumentation, if it is required, and the plastic presentation on paper of the finished work.

If, as regards the general conception and execution of the work, the procedure is more or less identical with all composers, it is far from being uniform in all that concerns the thematic conception and the disposition of the various elements. One musician has

to await patiently the blossoming of his ideas;
another, on the contrary, will endeavour to force
their coming with violence and excitation; a third—
like Beethoven—will write in feverish haste an in-
credible number of different sketches of a single
musical thought; a fourth—Bach, for instance—
will not give his theme plastic shape until it is
absolutely established in his own mind.

"Father" Franck was of those who, like Gluck
and many others, required some excitant in order to
find his ideas. It was not, however, in artificial
stimulants that he sought his inspiration; he had
recourse to music itself.

How often we used to see him pounding away
on his piano in a jerky and continually increasing
fortissimo the overture to "Meistersinger," or something by Bach, Beethoven, or Schumann! After a
time, more or less prolonged, the deafening noise
sank to a murmur, then silence—the master had
found his idea.

All through his life, as far as was possible, Franck
had recourse to this method of invoking inspiration
by musical noise, and one day, while composing his
last works, one of his pupils caught him struggling
with some pianoforte piece which he was ruthlessly
murdering. The student expressed some surprise at
his musical selection, whereupon the master replied:
" Oh, this is only just to work me up a little. When

I really want to find something good I play through *The Beatitudes;* that helps me better than anything."

Franck possessed two faculties invaluable to a composer : first, the power of carrying on two musical occupations at once without one suffering from the other ; secondly, the gift, more precious than all others, of being able to take up his work just where he had left off without needing an interval in which to get into the way of it again.

It often happened, in the course of his lessons— about which, however, he was extremely conscientious—that he would jump up and write down in a corner of his room a few bars that he did not want to forget, after which he would come straight back to his pupil and go on with the demonstration or examination in which they were engaged. Important works were written in this way, in fragments jotted down here and there ; and yet they kept a logical and unbroken sequence. It was the disposition of his ideas with which he was most preoccupied ; for, as I have already observed, while remaining a follower of classical tradition, he thirsted all his life after new forms, not only in the structure, but in the constituent elements of a work. Unlike Beethoven, whose thematic or elementary sketches are innumerable, but who, his themes once found, seems by this fact alone able to map out the whole development of a composition, so that he often neglects to note its progress in his sketch-books, Franck set down in pencil and rubbed out many pages before he definitely settled the disposition of a work.

Very critical of others as regards musical structure, he was still more severe towards himself, and when he was in doubt as to the choice of a relative key, or the progress of some development, he liked to consult his pupils, to make them understand his perplexity and ask their advice.

Following nature's law which—whatever we may say to the contrary—demands that the majority of composers who live long enough should pass through three phases of expression, we find in César Franck's music three clearly defined styles, each of which corresponds to some external change in his life, and is representative of his fullest development in that particular phase of which it is the perfect flower, because it displays all its characteristic features while it synthetises this particular phase as regards form.

I divide the master's career into three periods. The first, extending from 1841 until 1858, includes the four *Trios*, the fugitive pieces for piano, and a number of vocal melodies. This period culminates in his first oratorio, *Ruth*.

The second period extends from 1858 to 1872, and is the period of his sacred music, masses, motets, organ pieces, &c. ; it ends with his second oratorio, *Redemption*.

His third style embraces all his orchestral music from 1875 onwards, the admirable examples of chamber music, the two operas, the last chorales, and is crystallised in the sublime epic *The Beatitudes*.

These three periods I now wish to lay before my readers in an historical and analytical review, as succinct as possible, of the master's principal works.

IV

FIRST PERIOD (1841–1858)

THERE was a time—long gone by—when red-hot Wagnerians went into convulsions if any one ventured to say in their presence that the art of " Tannhäuser " and " The Flying Dutchman" was at all inferior to that of " Tristan " or " Parsifal." This is still the way— and always will be—with people of preconceived ideas who will not, or cannot, reason out their opinions. For my own part, I cannot help seeing something touching in this tendency to idolise men of genius or talent, although it does not assist the ends of justice. In any case, as I am now undertaking to write a criticism, I must refrain from passing judgments which are influenced by the affection I shall always feel for my lamented master. Such judgments are bound to be partial; therefore I shall have the courage to say that although Franck's first manner presents some extremely interesting peculiarities, it was far from foretelling all the grandeur, novelty, and sublimity that the master's art was eventually to bring forth.

In this first period, apart from certain typical compositions, Franck's personality is to a great extent absorbed by external influences : that of Beethoven in the *Trios ;* of Liszt and the romantic school in the pianoforte pieces ; finally, of Méhul and the French school of the late eighteenth century in all the vocal compositions. These influences are particularly noticeable in his general melodic style and the disposition of his works ; as regards synthetic rhythm and musical structure, the chief features of his two later styles, they hardly exist in this first period. It is with surprise that we see much more clearly a kind of embarrassment and timidity in the construction of most of these works, which results in downright monotony, and even becomes the cause of defects that Franck would never have tolerated thirty years later in his pupils.

There are, however, certain exceptions to this rule. I have already called attention to one—the first *Trio* in F sharp, which is all the more remarkable because the master described this work as forming part of his Op. 1. I am inclined to think, however, although I am not in a position to prove it, that several pianoforte pieces and a number of songs are anterior to the *Trio* in question.

Op. 1 was published under the following title : *Trois trios concertans pour piano, violon et violoncelle, dédiés à Sa Majesté Léopold I., roi des Belges, par*

César-Auguste Franck, de Liège. The first edition was issued by Schuberth and Co. (Hamburg and Leipzig), at the price of 3 *reichsthäler* (about 9s. 6d.), the composer retaining the rights in the work for France.

The *Trio* in F sharp is built upon two principal cyclic themes, of which the first serves as basis for all three movements of the work, and engenders in its various transformations the greater part of the developments ; while the second, which is unmodified, is fully reproduced in each movement.

If it were permissible to attribute a romantic origin to the work, we might say that the first theme strives by means of intricate snares and subtle transformations to draw the second into its restless circumventions ; but the latter holds out to the end by the sole strength of its simple and serene purity.

The first of these generative themes is of the complex nature demanded by the activity of the part it plays ; it necessitates a counterpoint which, whether it accompanies the subject or moves independently, becomes one of the most active agents in the thematic structure of the work :

The opening movement is in the form of an
Andante, and consists of five sections, or compartments,
which are only a series of expositions of the two
germinal ideas, theme A being the subject of the
first, third, and fourth sections, while the melodic
theme B :

the subject of the second and fifth sections, brings in
the key of F sharp major, in which the work closes.
In this early effort Franck already shows his pre-
dilection for those sharp keys which afterwards
supplied him with the subject-matter of such lofty
inspirations.

It should be observed that this *Andante,* conforming
to the old Italian style, only modulates by a change
of mode ; it is therefore—and the composer intended
it to be—a simple exposition of the two musical
personalities which play their parts in the succeeding
movements.

The second movement, in the subdominant (B

minor), presents the type of the great *Scherzo*-form, with two *Trios*, and follows step by step in the tracks of Beethoven's tenth and fourteenth quartets, with this peculiarity—that the second *Trio*, the culminating-point of the movement, is formed by the generative theme B, upon a rhythm which has already been heard in the opening *Andante*, and has also been used as the principal subject of the first *Trio* :

Like the preceding *Andante*, the *Scherzo* only modulates by a simple change of mode, but after some ingenious developments furnished by the combination of the counter-subject *a*, and afterwards the theme A, with the subject proper of the movement, it runs straight into the overwhelming *Finale*

in F sharp major, the chief melody of which, in all its generous simplicity, is only an expressive amplification of the first generative theme (A). In the same way, by a most logical symmetry, the second subject of this *Finale,* given out in D flat major (for C sharp, the dominant) is heard above continuous *pizzicati* for violoncello, the rhythm being that of the counter-subject *a.*

This *Finale* is in first-movement form (sonata-form), and its development, which advances steadily towards the light, offers some curious simultaneous associations of ideas peculiar to the *Finale* itself with the theme A and the counter-melody *a ;* it culminates in an almost dramatic episode in D major which leads to the recapitulation.

By way of crowning the work, the primitive theme returns, intact and immaculate, winding up triumphantly in the key of F sharp major. This last movement is the only one of the three which shows those gradations of colour due to tonal combinations, which Franck afterwards used to such good purpose.

If I have dwelt long upon the analysis of this work, it is because—in spite of the poverty of literary language to describe music—it was important to show how far Franck's art is allied to that of the latest sonatas and quartets of Beethoven.

We may pass lightly over the Second and Third *Trios.* The former (in B flat major), which is very much influenced by Weber and Schubert, and labelled by the composer himself with the odd and restrictive title of *Trio de Salon*, has few points of interest beyond a few rhythmical experiments in the *Andante*, and more particularly in the *Finale*. As to the third *Trio* in B minor, the developments of which are more concise than those of the two earlier examples, I cannot conscientiously compare it with the work I have just been analysing as far as its leading ideas are concerned. The *Finale*, composed much later than the other movements (further on I give the reason for this), is the only one of them which offers in its Beethoven-like spirit some curious alternations of rhythm and ingenious combinations.

The Fourth Trio (Op. 2), also in B minor, is dedicated *To my friend Fr. Liszt*, and the French rights are in the hands of the publisher Schlésinger. It has a history, which our master frequently related to us.

In 1842 young César Franck, who, as we saw in the first chapter of this book, had been obliged to leave the Paris Conservatoire, was in Brussels, where Liszt, then in the heyday of his fame as a virtuoso, was astounding all the drawing-rooms and carrying away the hearts of all the ladies. The great pianist, who showed himself all through life extremely well disposed towards his brother musicians—a rare virtue in the artistic world—and above all towards those who seemed to him endowed with genuine artistic feeling, did not disdain to receive the young composer of twenty with affability when he came to show him his first attempts.

The three *Trios* interested him enormously. He was exceedingly enthusiastic over the *Finale* of the third (in B minor), and told Franck that this movement seemed to him complete in itself and worthy of being published separately, and that, in this form, he would make a point of playing it and making it known in Germany.*

Young Franck lost no time in conforming to the advice of his illustrious friend ; he cut out the *Finale* of the last *Trio* from his Op. 1, and replaced it by the one with which the work now concludes.

This is why the *Fourth Trio*, Op. 2, consists only of a single movement in sonata-form in which the expositions are inverted, so that the last begins by delivering the *second theme*, keeping the initial phrase for the end. In spite of the incontestable value of this work, we might complain that the first idea was over-extended and the second too concise, which, in spite of a system of compensation, is far from resulting in general harmony and balance.

---

* Liszt kept his promise, as we may see in the interesting "Memories of a Musical Life," by Dr. Mason, of New York, who worked with Liszt from 1850 to 1854. Mason kept a diary during his stay in Weimar, from which the following extract is quoted : "Sunday, April 24, 1853, at the Altenburg, 11 A.M. Liszt played two *Trios* by César Franck with Laub and Cossmann " (p. 122).

Apart from this defect, the work is quite in the master's inspired style, and very superior to the two earlier *Trios*.

It was not performed in France until January 25, 1879, when it was given for the first time at one of the concerts of the Société Nationale de Musique by MM. Delaborde, Paul Viardot, and J. Griset.

Liszt remembered César Franck, always met him again with pleasure, and never ceased to admire him. Besides his opinion on the organ pieces, of which I will speak later on, I know that he warmly recommended the music of our French master to German artists, and I remember the delight and friendly enthusiasm with which he received the score of *Redemption*, which Franck charged me to take to him in Weimar, on my first visit to Germany in 1873. In this respect he was very different to Brahms, for whom I had to undertake the same commission; for he laid the book down on some piece of furniture with an air of supreme boredom, without so much as glancing at the reverential dedication which our dear, good Franck had inscribed on the first page.

Of all the vocal works composed by Franck between 1840 and 1853, the most beautiful, and certainly the most spontaneous, is the setting of Reboul's verses " *L'Ange et l'Enfant.*" I think it would be difficult to find a more intimate communion of

thought between poet and musician ; Franck's angel
(the earliest of all his angelic presentments) is truly the
guardian angel of the Catholic faith, watching tenderly
over the soul of the little child, joyfully sheltering
it from earthly dangers and bearing it aloft in un-
stained innocence to its heavenly home. This song,
which does not call into requisition a single strange
harmony, or even a modulation, is really a little masterpiece of expressive melody, such as we should be glad
to meet with more often in music. It dates from
1846.

Passing on to the pianoforte pieces, I must first
point out a curious fact which, as far as I know, is
quite peculiar to the composer with whom we are
dealing ; namely, that his works in this sphere may
be portioned out very exactly between the beginning
and close of his career.

Between 1841 and 1846, the first six years of his
creative activity, we find, apart from the *Trios*,
scarcely anything but pianoforte works, amounting
in all to fourteen. Then, quite suddenly, Franck
ceased writing for the instrument beloved of Chopin
and Liszt, and it was not until forty years later, at
the close of his life, and during another period of
six years—from 1884 until his death—that he began
to be haunted by a wish to invent new formulas
applicable to the keyboard instrument, and not only

succeeded in finding them, but was led on as it were by destiny to the discovery of æsthetic forms, hitherto unknown, which resulted in those perfect musical types which none of his successors has yet turned to good account.

But we have not yet come to the superb productions of his last style, and at present I must confine myself to the works belonging to the early years of his artistic career.

The first pianoforte pieces, which are also the master's earliest essays in composition, date as far back as 1835, when Franck was thirteen, and are to be found at the end of a manuscript book, extremely neat as regards writing, containing all the exercises he did under Reicha, from June 24, 1835, to May 15, 1836. These exercises show that Reicha taught him harmony and counterpoint *conjointly*.*

After numerous attempts at melodic construction upon themes given by the teacher, we find on one of the last pages this triumphant headline: "Songs by *me*, to be accompanied," above several little melodies which are actually the first authentic compositions set down by the author of the *Quartet in D major*.

---

* This manuscript is in the possession of M. Ch. Malherbe, the erudite archivist of the Opera, who very kindly permitted me to see it and to copy the little piece quoted above. In the Library at Boston, U.S.A., is another of Franck's manuscript books, but it contains no attempts at composition.

Half-way through the book there is an ingenuous reference to the death of the professor who had so far guided the master's first steps in his art.* I cannot resist the pleasure of quoting one of these naïve melodies :

4 Octobre
1835

<small>* This reference, which occurs again in almost identical terms at the end of the book, runs as follows : " M. Reicha, my professor, who wrote the preceding maxims, died on May 26, 1836, rue du Mont Blanc, 50, Paris.   May 27th, 1836.   César-Auguste Franck."</small>

Of all the other pianoforte works of this period, only two seem to me worthy of mention, on account of the very advanced experiments in instrumental forms which they contain. The first is entitled *Eclogue*, Op. 3, and bears the sub-title of *Hirten-Gedicht* (" Shepherd's Song ") ; it is dedicated to Baroness Chabannes, and was published in 1842, by Schlésinger. The exposition of the phrase in E minor—the " Shepherd's Song "—gives rise to some curious combinations of pianistic writing, which we shall rediscover in the pieces of his latest period.

Like Weber, Franck had very large hands ; consequently he often writes chords which demand a great stretch between the thumb and little finger. On account of these stretches it was difficult to write certain passages on two staves, especially when, as in

the *Eclogue*, there is a melody to be divided between
both hands ; a melody, moreover, which it is not
very easy to pick out among the swarms of notes and
chords with which it is surrounded.   At this period
Liszt alone had ventured to write pianoforte music on
three staves, but unknown composers, such as the
young César-Auguste, were not authorised by the
publishers to take any such licence; therefore the
execution of these pieces of Franck's becomes at times
extremely arduous, on account of the way in which
they are printed.   How much clearer to the reader
the frequent statements of the second theme would
have appeared in this form :

The second interesting piece is the first *Ballade*,
Op. 9, dating from 1844.   It must have been published, but it is now impossible to buy it, or even to
find a trace of it in any of the publishing houses

which succeeded those existing in 1844. No copy
was sent to the Bibliothèque Nationale, nor to the
library of the Conservatoire ; the manuscript alone
has been preserved in the master's family, and belongs
to M. Georges C. Franck. The work is written in
the key of B major, to which " Father " Franck was
particularly partial; a tonality invariably favourable to
his inspiration, from the *Trios* to the sublime *Larghetto*
of the *Quartet.*

After an introduction of forty-nine bars the *Ballade*
opens with a series of statements in single notes, of a
theme the naïve mood of which recurs in the works
of Franck's maturity. To this succeeds an *Allegro* in
B minor, of which the highly pianistic forms only
tend to a discreet inflexion to the key of the dominant,
leading back to a restatement of the primitive theme
ornamented by semiquavers, according to the formula
then in general use.

It is interesting to note, in this connection, that all
the master's early pianoforte works, without exception,
be they called eclogue, ballade, caprice, or fantasia,
are all written on one and the same plan : an *Allegro*
enclosed between two statements of the same theme,
sometimes preceded by a brief introduction. They
are, moreover, rendered rather monotonous by the
entire lack of modulation (to which we have already
called attention in the *Trios*); but, on closer examination, we may discover in them the embryonic forms

of the great works of later years, and the anxiety to write brilliantly for the instrument is not so intense that it does not often give way to the pursuit of purely musical forms. Obviously at this period Franck, who was urged by his father to produce "saleable pieces" at any price, did not understand that art of composition which he afterwards taught so thoroughly; therefore the future master of modern musical structure, being well aware of his inferiority, prudently restricted himself to a simple form which offered no pitfalls. Later on he took his revenge !

The same remarks apply to *Ruth*, a Biblical eclogue, dating from 1843, and only published by Hartmann in 1871.

The fresh and ingenuous melodies of this work, so evidently the outcome of his frequent study of Méhul's works, often reveal a certain originality to those who know Franck's music as a whole; but the forms are still tentative and confused, and sometimes show a timidity which not only surprises us, but even provokes a smile.

The phrase for violin in G minor with which the Prelude opens is very closely allied in outline to one of the themes in the first *Trio;* it is already the earliest lisping of the true Franckian melody :

Ruth.

1er Trio
(Final)

The first part of the oratorio, describing the departure of Naomi, is constructed upon sombre tonalities which are very appropriate to the situation. Only Ruth's generous resolution, when she exclaims that she will not leave her mother, but will follow her everywhere, sounds a brighter note by establishing the key of A major, which comes like a streak of sunshine lighting up the preceding gloom. Unfortunately the air sung by Ruth is essentially too *operatic*, and its opening melody is more reminiscent of Meyerbeer's dramatic songs than predictive of the creator of *Redemption*.

In the second part, after various Choruses of the Reapers, which were our admiration at twenty, followed by a kind of sad melopœia for Naomi, in which the continuous line of the cor anglais recalls too often a certain well-known passage in Halévy's "La Juive," we come to a duet between Ruth and Boaz which is to my mind the culminating-point in all the melody written by Franck during his first period of development, and at the same time a page of real interest as regards dramatic expression.

The simple dialogue, very much resembling that of the scenes between Jacob and Benjamin in Méhul's " Joseph," is continuously intertwined with a pure melodic line :

the effect being somewhat like that of the arrangement of certain draperies in the frescoes of Orcagna or Botticelli. The sweet and clinging musical phrase moves in, or near to, the key of B flat major, and ends with Ruth's confident exclamation :

Ah ! je ne suis plus étrangère !

which, indicating an emotional change in the young Moabite, introduces, according to the principles of dramatic construction, an entirely new tonality bearing no relationship to the one which has so far predominated ; this is the wholly radiant key of B major, in which the first section is now repeated, and the scene ends.

The third part contains a second duet for Ruth and Boaz, similar to the one of which I have just spoken, which is one of the most truly Franckian numbers in the score.

In connection with this scene it is interesting to observe the variety of impressions which can be produced by one and the same melodic outline : one of the chief motives, which is used here to depict the paternal tenderness of Boaz, is identical in design with a theme employed by M. Massenet to express

the somewhat unhealthy passion of Des Grieux for
the lively Manon :

and yet, in spite of the fact that the succession of notes is the same, how different the impression!

There could be nothing more calmly chaste than the melody forming the basis of the final number in *Ruth*, which, starting in D major, eventually brings back the luminous colouring of B major, a tonality that has already made its appearance in the duet in the second part.

Thus, in the score of *Ruth* Franck has summed up the fullest capacities of his first stage of development, as much by the musical importance of the work as by its dramatic tendency, which was quite a new feature in his work.

We shall now see how entirely he abandoned this course in order to soar completely above it into fresh artistic spheres.

V

SECOND PERIOD (1858–1872)

W ITH the commencement of this second period we
are confronted with a chronological problem, the
solution of which continues to present some difficulties.

At the outset of his career, instigated in all
probability by his father, Franck carefully catalogued
everything that came from his pen with the sense of
order which never left him till the day of his death.
To each work he appended a number, upon which,
apparently, we might rely for a general classification.
And yet, in spite of this care, certain numbers
belonging to this period are surrounded with doubt,
such as the *Solo for Piano, accompanied by String
Quartet*, Op. 10, of which no vestige can be traced
either at his publishers' or in the memories of his
most intimate friends; and, again, the *Fantasia for
Pianoforte*, Op. 13, announced on the cover of the
Fantasias upon Gulistan (Richault, publisher), at the
same time as other works, " by the same composer,"
which I strongly suspect to have been advertised

but never written, or at any rate never sent to the engraver.

But the most curious thing in this connection, and one to which I desire to call attention at the beginning of my study of Franck's second manner, is the fact that the organ pieces, which are the first manifestations of his true innovating genius, bear the following opus numbers: 16, 17, 18, 19, 20, and 21. Now there is an earlier Op. 16—*Trois petits riens* ("Three Trifles") for piano; and also another Op. 17, the *Grand Duet for Four Hands on Lucile* (Richault), both these works dating from 1845. In the same way the *Mass for Three Voices* is labelled "Op. 12," and yet the same number was assigned in 1844 to the *Second Fantasia on Gulistan*, published by Richault.

Did Franck intend to repudiate some of his earlier pianoforte pieces, written under paternal pressure, as unworthy to figure in his artistic work? It is not impossible. Yet, at the same time, he permitted the existence of other compositions (the Duet on "God Save the King" and the *Souvenir of Aix-la-Chapelle*) which cannot have been in any way superior to the first-named. The question will never be solved.

On the other hand, none of the numerous *Mélodies*, composed and published between 1840 and 1850, bear opus numbers; and after the piece

entitled *Quasi Marcia*, for harmonium, numbered
Op. 22, the master abandoned the practice of
numeral designation.

In any case, the six great pieces for organ mark
the start of the symphonic production which characterises this second period. I lay stress on the word
symphonic because there is no doubt that a number
of motets and other sacred works, as well as the two
Masses, are anterior to this time; although we have
already seen that Franck was not in the habit of
numbering his vocal pieces.

We might call this second period in the life of
César Franck the period of religious composition.
With the exception of a few songs, an attempt at an
oratorio, and *Redemption*, this portion of his career
produced nothing but music intended for church
use.

Observe that I say *intended* for church use, not
actually church music, and this necessitates a few
words of explanation.

The origin of Music, like that of all the other
arts—although we vainly endeavour to refer them to
other causes—is to be found incontestably in religion.
The earliest song was a prayer. To praise God, to
celebrate the beauty, the joy, and even the terrors of
religion, was the sole object of all works of art for
nearly eight hundred years. In this way the artists
of those days gave expression to *life*, to men's

emotions, such as love, hope, joy, and grief, and we may say in passing that they expressed these things with far more depth and truth than do those who, under the pretext of *actuality*, can only give utterance to the superficial, futile, and fleeting side of existence.

The Renaissance, by a change of tendency which had its origin in an erroneous idea, gave us a few personal masterpieces ; but it caused a terrible upheaval in the logical progress of the Arts, and sacred music, more particularly, became from this time forth a kind of conventional art, which, abolishing all truth of expression, and disdaining the fine rhythm of the old monodies, and the harmonious architecture of vocal counterpoint, introduced into the church the symphonic style, or, worse still, a style which had no place, or reason, within the sacred precincts.

Thus church music, so-called, degenerated with appalling rapidity, and became merely the prey of convention and fashion.

In the seventeenth century it was pompous, following the etiquette of the Court of the Grand Monarch. In the eighteenth century it became frivolous, for the distraction of the people of quality, or the snobs who, on leaving a supper-party, felt bound by their social position to put in an appearance at church. Finally it became quite *bourgeois* and stagnated under the influence of ready-made formulæ

which characterised the reign of " the happy medium."
It was this last style, which lacked the dignity of the
seventeenth and the charm of the eighteenth centuries,
that lasted on to the close of the nineteenth ; and,
strange to relate, schools were actually formed for
the purpose of teaching young composers the art
of manufacturing expressionless music for church
purposes.

César Franck never really lost himself in those
shameful depths wherein lie the so-called *Kapellmeister*, or " choir-master's," compositions.   He was
incapable of such descents.   Nevertheless, in his
church music he could not entirely free himself
from the influences of his time, and after an im-
partial examination of his works we are compelled
to observe the strange fact that although he was
perhaps the only religious musician at the end of
the last century, yet his sacred music is undoubtedly
inferior to that which he accomplished in other
branches, orchestral, pianoforte, and chamber music.

There are two reasons for this.   In the first place,
Franck, who was so learned in all that concerns
modern music and that of the eighteenth century,
was very indifferently informed as regards the
admirable and monumental polyphonic schools of
France and Italy in the sixteenth century, editions
of which were rare and not very accessible in his
day.

He knew nothing about the erudite and definitive researches of the Benedictines into the subject of Gregorian music, and M. Charles Bordes, in an article written immediately after Franck's glorification,* was quite right when he characterised the master's position in the sphere of sacred music as follows :

"In his church music César Franck remains, with a few rare exceptions, a *soloist*. He stands upon the threshold of that *Dextera* the *ensemble* of which lives as a superb piece of pure music, but the initial phrase of which unfolds itself with the amplitude and majesty of certain statues seen in churches of the rococo style, of which it is impossible to deny the theatrical and anti-religious appearance.

"In his Mass, of which the *Kyrie* is an exquisite prayer and the *Agnus Dei* a gem of musical ingenuity, how shall we qualify the noisy *Quoniam tu solus sanctus*, which is less worthy of a soloist than of a chorister in rather a merry condition ? Side by side with these pages which do no credit to the master, we may place the incomparable opening of the offertory *Quæ est ista*, which is worthy of Bach, and the admirable *Domine non secundum*, with its counter-point of a very human kind, and—with the sole exception of the final *reprise* in the major, which only aims at effect—so sober that this motet might be cited as a model of modern church music.

* *Le Courrier Musical*, November 1, 1904.

" Pages such as these fill us with bitter regret that Franck started his career too soon to take part in our movement to reform sacred music. Knowing little of Palestrina, with whose beauties, as he informed me himself, he had only superficially come in contact, and whose religious appropriateness he did not appreciate, as with so many musicians of his generation, his interest stopped short at the writing and artifices of that style of composition. But what would he not have written for the Church if only his noble soul had once been awakened to all the serene beauty of the earlier masters! He would have continued to draw upon himself for his deepest emotional aspects, but, made wise by precept, he would not have overwhelmed us quite so much with his natural gifts. With his certainty of touch, what pure masterpieces he would have bestowed upon us, written from his intellect, it is true, but glowing with the movements of his charitable and loving soul!

" Probably he would have found it difficult not to look within himself and his own music for the elements of expression which would have tempered these liturgical formulæ, but what fine art-forms would have been the outcome of these conflicting influences, amid which Franck would have remained, in spite of all, just the divine *Pater seraphicus* whose ingenuousness and modesty were limitless!"

Another reason for the inferiority of Franck's church music is quite fortuitous. When he was appointed to the future basilica of Sainte-Clotilde it was not the rich parish church that it afterwards became. The funds were not sufficient for the purchase of music, having regard to the solemnity of the services. Thus, existing for the "ordinary" upon their repertory and old material, the clergy unconsciously followed the customs of the sixteenth and seventeenth centuries in counting upon the organist and choir-master to supply the necessary new music, and so add to the brilliancy of important parish ceremonies.

César Franck, like Bach and Palestrina, composed all the music that was required for the celebrations of great feast-days; but on account of the haste and exigencies of modern life he could not devote enough time to thinking out and writing fine works. Therefore, in spite of the indisputable beauties pointed out by M. Charles Bordes in the article we have quoted above, the master's religious music, which in consequence of his early training was not very liturgical, does not present, when judged from a true artistic standpoint, an interest at all proportionate to that which characterises his work in other styles.

Only his organ works, which are evidently destined for church purposes, but belong more to the symphonic order, survive amid the choral music, and will remain an imperishable monument to the art beloved of Frescobaldi and J. S. Bach.

It is with these compositions that I propose to start my review of the second period of my master's career.

With the appearance of the *Fantasia in C* we become aware of the true style of the composer of *The Beatitudes*.

If the construction of this piece—which is indeed fantastic, with its central point on the subdominant and its ending, somewhat curtailed, but full of charm—reminds us of the hesitations of his first manner, the *Lied* at the commencement, flowing along calmly and without modulation, shows us what eventually became the general characteristic of his third style which linked him so closely to the radical qualities of Beethoven, namely, the gift of evolving a living melody from a pre-established harmonic condition. (Compare the third Variation of the *Adagio* of Beethoven's Twelfth Quartet.) And if we reflect that, in its kind, this harmonic condition is itself the result of a melodic canon—a favourite device of Franck's—we shall have no difficulty in reconstituting by means of this example the table of affiliation to which I drew attention at the beginning of this chapter: to the early Italians for the purity

of his monodic line; to an unconscious reversion to
the polyphonic composers of the sixteenth century
for his easy mastery of counterpoint; to Bach for
his style of writing and to Beethoven for general
rhythmic disposition. If it were not that I regard
these comparisons as futile, I could even discover in
this piece the *prescience* of Wagner (at this moment
completely ignored in France), since the theme which
flows on the keyboard of the great organ from the
architectural combination of which I have spoken is
the one known by the label of the "motive of sleep"
in " Die Walküre " and throughout the whole epic
of the " Nibelungen."

In the *Grande Pièce Symphonique* we find ourselves
confronted, for the first time in the progress of the
master's work, with a true sonata, or rather a symphony, since it is the custom to describe in this way
a sonata coloured by various *timbres*.

This is the first of all those organ symphonies

which have since enriched modern music, and if I
may express my personal opinion, this way of composing symphonies by means of the numerous and
varied *timbres* of an organ by Cavaillé-Coll seems to
me far preferable to combining organ with orchestra.
These two forces do not agree, and the effect of the
juxtaposition of two similar forces is invariably the
overshadowing and weakening of the one for the
useless profit of the other. Berlioz, the genius of
the chemistry of *timbre*, had already called attention
to the uselessness of such a combination when he
wrote in his *Traité d'Orchestration*, with that imagery
which makes his writings so attractive : " The
orchestra is Emperor, the organ is Pope." It is
wiser not to revive in music the quarrel of the
" Investitures."

Franck did not commit this incongruity, which
was repugnant to his classical spirit ; * therefore his
Grande Pièce, in F sharp minor, is really a symphony
in three movements, and displays all the characteristics of this form of composition : the first movement is built on two ideas in sonata-form, preceded
by an introduction which reappears in the course of

---

* Not one of the old masters employed the combination of
organ and orchestra in equal strength. Bach scarcely ever wrote
for organ *solo* with orchestra, except as a harmonic realisation. As
to Handel's concertos, the string quartet and the oboes play but
a very secondary part in them.

the development ; the *Andante* is in *Lied*-form, the
second section of which, by reason of its rapid *tempo*,
may be regarded as taking the place of a *Scherzo*
(the composer returned to this plan of construction
later on, in his *Symphony in D*) ; the *Finale* is led up
to by a recapitulation of the chief ideas which have
been previously exposed, its principal theme being
identical with that of the first movement, now given
out in F sharp major, like an apotheosis, and developed by means of fugal devices until the conclusion is reached. The whole work is connected
by one leading idea.

The third piece, *Prelude, Fugue, and Variation* in
B minor, dedicated to Saint-Saëns, is so well known
by the arrangement made by the composer himself for
harmonium and piano that I need not dwell upon it.
It is only necessary to observe that it contains in
embryo the new forms which he afterwards elaborated
in his last pianoforte compositions.   Nor should we
fail to notice the musical charm of the fugue, which
is very different from the insipid class-room fugues,
the only kind being written at that time.

The *Pastorale* in *Lied*-form which follows also
presents this special feature of a fugal development
possessing real charm and melody which is the
logical fulfilment of the system indicated in
Beethoven's third period.

The last two pieces, *Prière* in C sharp, and *Finale*

in B flat major, both approximate to first-movement form. The latter is particularly interesting on account of its firm, Beethoven-like structure; its graceful second theme contrasting with the inflexibility of the first; and also because of the important development toward the close, which leads to a forceful and majestic peroration.

These organ works, so different from the purely show-pieces of Lefébure-Wély and other organists of that day, so lofty as regards inspiration, so perfect in workmanship, will remain a solid monument and mark a memorable date in the history of the myriad-voiced instrument. Nor can we doubt that every one possessed of the artistic spirit will share Liszt's enthusiasm, who, coming down from the organ-loft where Franck had just been playing these compositions to him, exclaimed with sincere emotion: "These poems have their place beside the master-pieces of Sebastian Bach!"

I must now speak of the *Mass for Three Voices*, first performed on April 2, 1861. It is undoubtedly of earlier date than the organ pieces with which we have just been dealing; but I was particularly anxious to make these the point of departure of Franck's second style, and by way of excuse for this violation of chronological order I can affirm that the Mass was so often revised between 1859 and 1872 that it may be said to spread itself over the whole of the second period, and to display in its widely discrepant numbers those phases of transformation which we find in all geniuses during their middle period of production.

The work was specially written for the church of Sainte-Clotilde, shortly after the composer had been appointed organist there. The *Kyrie, Gloria,* and *Sanctus* even go back to the time when he was only the choir-master of the basilica, M. Théodore Dubois, the future Director of the Conservatoire, being organist and accompanist.* On the other hand, the *Credo* belongs to a more recent date, and some years later still the soaring *Agnus Dei* replaced another *Agnus* which did not satisfy the master, who completely destroyed it. As regards the *Panis Angelicus,* which has passed under a multitude of disguises into the repertory of organists and choir-masters, it was only interpolated into the Mass in 1872, when the work was published by the firm of Repos, in the Rue Bonaparte.

Of the *Kyrie,* a sweet and simple prayer, and the *Gloria,* certain passages of which are really vulgar and unworthy of the composer of *The Beatitudes,* I will say nothing. They belong to the category of what it was then customary to describe as sacred music because it was hung on to a Latin text.

* See M. Théodore Dubois' speech on the occasion of the inauguration of the Franck monument, October 22, 1904.

THE BASILICA CHURCH OF SAINTE-CLOTILDE
(Showing the monument to Franck in the garden)

The *Credo*, which is far more and far better worked out, has the peculiar feature of being written in first-movement form, the exposition being in C minor, leading to a second subject in G major at the words *Et incarnatus est*, the scene of Calvary and the Resurrection being treated as developments of the initial theme.   But when the exposition is repeated a modified version of the second subject replaces the first in the progression of the sonata, at the words *Et in spiritum sanctum*, and continues its final development at considerable length until it returns in its first form, thus characterising the formula of Christian hope, *Exspecto resurrectionem mortuorum*, and ending with the *Amen* in C major, a key which has predominated almost exclusively from the start of the recapitulation.

In spite of the beauties of this *Credo*, it must be confessed that the use of a familiar and definite symphonic form is not very happy in its results, although we acknowledge attempts at a mystical and sometimes deeply religious expression—such, for instance, as the association in one and the same musical idea of the Incarnation, the union of the human and divine personality, with the Resurrection of the body, that mysterious conquest of the divine essence by human matter.

The *Sanctus* flows simply and serenely, like the *Kyrie*, with a brief stress upon the *Hosanna*, after

which it relapses into melancholy at the *Benedictus*.
The *Agnus Dei* is a little masterpiece of concision and
melodious tenderness. After the threefold invocation
in A minor, C major, and E minor, the sopranos, as
though carried away by some sublime hope, sing a
hymn of peace, while the basses continue to re-
echo the theme of the previous invocation, and the
number ends with a *pianissimo* for the three voices
unaccompanied, which seems to take us to the
threshold of some mystic *janua cæli*.

When I said in the opening chapter of this book
that Franck was Beethoven's continuator, not merely
in the sphere of symphony, which is indisputable,
but also in that of religious music, I had the *Agnus
Dei* and *Kyrie* of the Mass in my mind. Not that
I wish to compare the modest work of the choir-
master of Sainte-Clotilde—a work which was written
in all sincerity, but to utilitarian ends—with that
effulgent epic of divine suffering and human aspira-
tion, the *Missa Solemnis*, which I regard as the most
perfect of the creations of the Titan of Symphony.
Nor do I pretend to place the sweet, confiding *Dona
nobis pacem* of the Mass we are analysing in the same
rank with the breathless, incomparable appeal for
peace which rises amid the distant sounds of war in
the dramatic *Agnus Dei* of Beethoven. But it seems
as though, in spite of the musical inequality of the
two works, the spirit of one must have passed into

the spirit of the other with less forceful human expression, but with more divine confidence.

Do we not find, to begin with, the same fundamental error which causes the Mass in D minor— one of the most sublime monuments in music—to stand quite outside the liturgical framework of true church music by reason of its dramatic tendency? Do we not find the same somewhat conventional pomp and grandiloquence employed precisely in the same places? But, on the other hand, without wishing to draw a useless æsthetic parallel between these two works, may we not say that if Franck falls into the same mistakes as his great ancestor as regards the liturgy itself, his Mass approaches more closely in certain passages of the *Kyrie, Sanctus,* and particularly in the *Agnus Dei,* to what must be considered as the legitimate style of church music? It is in this sense that I have ventured to point to Franck as Beethoven's continuator in sacred music, because, starting from the same conventional procedure, the composer of the *Mass for Three Voices* seems to be striving for a development which never comes to completion in his church music, but shows its full results in his oratorios and symphonic works.

Franck's Mass is, however, an unequal work, and M. Ricciotto Canudo, an Italian critic, is not altogether unjust when he makes the following criticism :

" The sweet and luminous *Kyrie* makes us think of a paradise of distant lights and far-away music ; it is a profound and beautiful expression of prayer, like the *Agnus* in the same Mass. But side by side with these is an almost commonplace *Gloria*, lacking in melodic idea and crushed by the noisy, dynamic preponderance of the instruments. Full of inequalities, the Mass, like all Franck's music, is a curious dream, half mystic, half secular, in which the flow of ecstatic sentiment is sometimes complete and superb, and sometimes interrupted by rhythms and affectations which are essentially theatrical." *

The most important work belonging to Franck's second style, the one which sums up all the qualities and defects of this period, is undoubtedly *Redemption*, an oratorio disguised by its authors under the singular title of a *Poem-Symphony*—a very inappropriate designation for a composition of this kind, which is neither a symphony nor a poem.

The subject, which, in spite of the rather ordinary versification of Edouard Blau, is not lacking in grandeur, sets forth the material and the spiritual redemption ; the first effected by Christ's coming upon earth, the second won during future ages by

* " César Franck e la giovane nuova scuola musicale francese," by Ricciotto Canudo ; extract from the *Nuova Antologia*, April 1, 1905.

means of prayer. This conception was quite in harmony with Franck's ideas, who willingly discoursed on this subject, emphasising his discourse with warmth and enthusiasm.

As to the music, having watched its evolution day by day, I shall endeavour to speak of it with justice and sincerity in spite of the natural partiality we feel for the child we have known from its birth.

This oratorio has a history, and I think the details which I can give *de visu* will be read with interest, and will be both instructive to composers and a lesson to their pupils.

No sooner had Franck received the text than, laying aside *The Beatitudes*, upon which he had already made a start, he threw himself into the musical realisation of the poem with such ardour that in spite of the small amount of time he could devote to the task, the work was finished in six months.

It is advisable to explain at this juncture the existence of two versions of *Redemption*, differing very considerably from each other. If the second offers a fine chorus and the admirable symphonic interlude which now forms part of the repertory of most concerts, the first, it must be confessed, was obviously superior as regards the general plan of the work, which was constructed upon a perfectly novel basis, such as only Franck could have conceived and realised.

In order to make this plan understood, I must give an outline of the poem :

Part I. Men move amid the egotistical darkness of paganism ; they think to find happiness in enjoyment and hatred, which bring forth only the works of death. Suddenly space is illuminated by a flight of angels, one of whom announces redemption through the Saviour's coming upon earth, and regenerate humanity unites in a Christmas hymn.

Part II. Symphonic Interlude. (Here I give the argument of the poem for the orchestra only, as it was imagined and revised by Franck himself). " Centuries pass. The joy of the world transformed and flourishing by the word of Christ. The era of persecution is started in vain, Faith triumphs over all obstacles. But now the modern period has come ! Belief has perished, and mankind, once more possessed by a cruel lust of enjoyment, and vain agitations, returns to the passions of the earlier ages."

Part III. The angels, covering their faces with their wings at the sight of the crimes committed upon earth, weep for men, who have reverted to pagan depravity. But the Archangel in a graver tone proclaims a new Redemption : the pardon of sins may be won by prayer. Mankind, at peace and repentant, unite heart and soul in a hymn of brotherly love.

Struck by the alternations of light and shade of which this poem admits, Franck believed that a well-established gradation of those musical tints we call *tonalities* would alone suffice, by means of opposition and contrast, to render the various shades of colour so clearly suggested by the text. He therefore thought out a tonal structure modelled absolutely

upon the meaning of the words, proceeding in the
first and second parts from darkness to light, while
the symphonic interlude, faithfully interpreting his
argument, should begin with a full warmth and glow
and end in the cold and lifeless tonality chosen for
the opening chorus of the work.

It was the first occasion upon which the master in
his search for poetic expression consciously applied
this fertile and traditional principle of tonal architecture, which he had hitherto used in a tentative
way, but which afterwards became the most forcible
element of his teaching.

I will give a brief analysis of the work, that my
readers may have some precise notion of the inspired
logic which guided his method of composition.

Part I.   A   short   introduction, foreshadowing
at an almost imperceptible distance the prophetic
song of the angels, the suave melody of which is
given out *pianissimo* by means of a canon in the tenth
below, and in the key of A major:

After this rough sketch, the key of A minor is
abruptly introduced, creating a sombre atmosphere

in which we discern, swarming and howling, all the vilest passions of the heathen world. Here, for the first time, we must make a remark which will have a still more striking application to *The Beatitudes :* the unfortunate musician goads himself in vain in his endeavours to express evil and moral hideousness such as his own simple beauty of character forbade him to conceive. Consequently this first chorus shows us the delights of paganism in a somewhat turgid and conventional light ; we never get out of the key of A minor, and the number ends in a *stretto* which is more noisy than powerful, according to the custom of the operas of that period.

After this all grows luminous, and the radiant prophetic theme soars majestically above human misery. This time it is delivered by the chorus in E major, the dominant of the key of the prelude, while the violins repeat the melody like an echo. This use of *canon*, already noticeable in his organ pieces, becomes more and more frequent in Franck's music, of which it may be said to be the hall-mark. But it differs from the kind of scholastic canon, too often substituted for the spirit of Bach, because the melody suitable to imitation is never twisted and deformed to fit the exigencies of the case, but is always simple and natural in its modulations, and the imitation flows along in so logical a way that it seems a mere addition.

After a few brief and hesitating answers from mankind which bring back the sombre tones of doubt, the prophecy of the Archangel bursts forth, preceding another exposition of the theme in A major, and progressing towards the light until we reach a dazzling modulation in F sharp major, which marks the triumphant entry of the melody long sought by the composer, whereby he personifies the idea of redemption.

This having been established, and Faith and Love having shone upon the earth, all becomes immovably fixed, and the men's voices are heard, repudiating their hatreds and gathering strength in this new tonality (F sharp major) preparatory to singing " Noël " at the cradle of the Infant Divinity.

The *Symphonic Interlude* which formed the second part of the work, and of which no traces now remain —except, perhaps, in the hands of a few collectors who were prudent enough to preserve the first edition— was far from equal to the number now known by this title. It was not, however, lacking in musical interest. After a short introduction the violas and violoncellos gave out a joyous theme in A major :

and soon afterwards a more tender subject, exposed at considerable length in F major :

The piece was subsequently developed in sonata-form, and, in the course of development, gravitating around C major as a central point, the rhythm and figures previously employed to depict the vileness of the heathen seemed to creep in, somewhat timidly at first. After the restatement of the two themes in A and C major, the melody of redemption established itself as a final exposition, descending from the highest orchestral groups to the basses in the triumphant tonality of F sharp major. Presently it modulated to the less luminous key of A major, as though to mingle with the initial joy of mankind ; but the latter, refusing the divine goodness, plunge once more into discord and egotism, and the piece ended with a brief restatement of the pagan theme, which is lost in the distance amid the glooms evoked by the key of A minor.

The poetic and musical basis of this orchestral interlude was really admirable ; the only thing to be regretted—apart from some rather tedious moments in the course of its execution—was the fact that the intrinsic value of the two fundamental themes was not quite equal to the loftiness of the subject they were intended to express.

Franck felt this himself, and in rewriting the piece from the first to the last bars he did well.

The third part was the same as we now know it, with the exception of the opening chorus, which had no place in the original scheme, for reasons which I will presently explain. The angels, taking flight from rebellious earth, sing sadly, and, as on the first occasion, the violins repeat their song in a melancholy echo ; but although constructed in the same style as the first, and noticeably allied to it melodically, this chorus gives quite a different impression. The angels do not weep with *human* feeling, as they rejoiced in the first chorus. To express their angelic sorrow Franck has found a melody which is both plaintive and serene, a sublime chant of pity suited to these immaterial beings. Only he himself could have discovered this melody.

The chorus is written in F sharp minor, thus contrasting with the gladness of Christmastide in the first part by the mere change of mode.

Gradually the light which has been extinguished for a time filters back through the darkness of human error. Hope reappears with the Archangel in an air more classical in spirit than the enthusiastic hymn in the first part. Modulating from B minor to B major, it gradually introduces (in the latter key) the ardent prayer of repentant humanity, above which, soaring as it were between earth and heaven, the angels sing the joyous theme of prophecy.

If we have carefully followed the order of the keys which Franck employs in this work, we shall be convinced of the evident intention of their disposition, an intention which the composer made no effort to conceal, and of which he was very proud. "In this score," he used to say to us, "I have only used *sharp keys*, in order to render the luminous idea of Redemption."

How admirably logical is the succession of sharp keys in this work!

Starting with a neutral and colourless key, *A minor*, the first part is illuminated by degrees; as by a ladder, we seem to rise to the *greatest light* by means of E, the dominant, A major, and F sharp major.

The central symphonic number, carrying out its poetic significance, takes us downwards from the bright key of A major to the primitive obscurity of A minor; but the last part, which begins sadly in F sharp minor (the relative of the preceding bright tonality), is again penetrated with luminous tints, and ends triumphantly in B major, a definite key in absolute contrast with the gloom of A minor, of which we now perceive that the " Noël " in F sharp, in the first part, was only the dominant herald.

This solid architectural design, which made up a perfect and wonderfully balanced structure, was unfortunately modified in the second edition of the work—the only one now extant. It is the history of this modification which I am about to relate—not without some hesitancy, I must confess, for I myself am partly accountable for this regrettable change of plan, and it is, I believe, the sole cause of self-reproach in my relations with my respected master. The confession of my mistake will unburden my conscience of the remorse which has long pursued me—ever since, in fact, I have come to know what musical composition really is.

The first performance of *Redemption* took place on Thursday in Holy Week, April 10, 1873, at the Concert Spirituel at the Odéon, under the direction of Colonne. The rehearsals did not go off without some hitches. From the beginning it was evident that the orchestral parts had been so badly copied that it was necessary to pull up the players at every bar in order to correct the most glaring mistakes; a condition of things that invariably throws an orchestra into confusion and generally sets the musicians against a work. The rehearsal for *Redemption* was therefore broken off and all the parts sent back to poor Franck, who was much annoyed by this mishap.

The second rehearsal was at hand, and only two days remained in which to correct all these parts, and even to recopy some which were illegible. I was very well acquainted with the score, because, at my master's request, I had accompanied on the piano all the choral practices. I therefore proposed, with the assistance of my fellow workers, Henri Duparc and Camille Benoît, to undertake this task myself; an offer which he accepted very simply, having, indeed, no time in which to be responsible for it himself.

We little knew what we had undertaken, and from the beginning we were alarmed at the mere manual labour to be got through in so short a time. However, we started bravely, working in Duparc's room, he taking possession of the paste-pot, Benoît collating, and I taking charge of the copies. In one day and two nights, during which we were kept awake by Duparc's brandy and Benoît's puns, all was finished and laid on the desks of the orchestra at the appointed time. Unfortunately, for reasons on which I will not dwell, the two remaining rehearsals were so curtailed that there was no time to work at the symphonic interlude which formed the second part of the work, and it was simply decided to cut it out, to the great vexation of the composer, who had to look on at the ruthless overthrow of the beautiful and harmonious

structure so long and so lovingly pondered and
elaborated.

The final chorus of the first part almost shared
the same fate. The orchestra, disgusted by the
fingering necessary for the key of F sharp major,
and in accordance with the attitude generally
assumed by the executants of those days towards a
newcomer (Franck, alas! was making a public *début*
at fifty!), declared the final number impossible.
The composer promptly and energetically refused
to permit this further mutilation of the work;
consequently the performance suffered deplorably
from the ill-will of the players.

Redemption formed only the second half of the
programme, the first part being as follows:

Psalm : *Cæli enarrant*	*Saint-Saëns*
Air from the *Stabat Mater*	*Mme. de Grandval*
Two airs with chorus from *Fiesque*	*E. Lalo*
Duet from the *Stabat Mater* .	*Rossini*

The performance of Franck's oratorio was poor.
The chorus did not always sing in tune, and Mme.
de Caters, who had only agreed to interpret the
"queer, ineffective music" of the Archangel on
condition that she should be consoled by some
taking *cantilena* of Rossini, bustled through her
part with perfunctory indifference. Consequently
the public did not understand the work at all, and

displayed their boredom so conspicuously that at the end of the concert only fifty people at most were left in the room.

Far more upset at the unfortunate defeat of our hopes than the composer himself, we, his pupils, set ourselves to account for the cause of it in the difficulties of execution which we thought to be the actual obstacle to a suitable performance of the work. Therefore we resolved to besiege the master with our objections until he consented to change the unlucky key of F sharp major, which we believed to be the source of all the evil.

I first undertook to broach the subject to him. I must own that I was not very well received on the first occasion, and, having sinned yet a second time, "Father" Franck, throwing aside his usual amenity, forbade me, with some severity, to mention the subject again. But after several of his favourite pupils, led by Henri Duparc, had returned to the attack, he ended by resigning himself to the transposition of the Archangel's aria and the whole of the last number of the first part into E major. But the entire design of the work was changed, for although it is easier to play in E major, this key is far from giving that effulgency which we derive from F sharp, which is the dominant, not the subdominant, of the final tonality.

To realise the difference, we need only compare the triumphal modulation in the first edition (p. 40):

with the corresponding page in the second edition, which appeared in 1875:

The orchestral interlude (*Symphony* it was called in the first edition) was also subjected to such numerous and important modifications, with which Franck was never satisfied, that he ended by entirely rewriting it on such different principles that he only followed the first edition in bringing back at the very end the central theme of the work, now transposed from B to D, and eventually leading to the peroration.

This entire remodelling of a long number, already engraved, which had cost its author so much trouble, is a curious example of the power of the artistic conscience ; but it is to this conscience that we owe the superb initial melody :

to which we cannot listen without emotion, since it is " music's self," as Chabrier said of it. This new number is in D major, and its poetic meaning is less complex than that of its predecessor, because it only attempts to depict " the joy of the world which is transformed and expanded by the words of Christ." It therefore remains tonal, and has no need of the dramatic change of key-colour towards darkness and obscurity, as in the original version. For this reason, wishing, however, to describe the condition of man when he returns to pagan disbelief,

Franck had to introduce as a counterfoil the male chorus in D minor which, in the second part, precedes the plaintive chorus of angels, and foreshadows a new style, the chief points of which we shall consider in the next chapter.

VI

THIRD PERIOD (1872–1890)

WE now find ourselves confronted with an entirely new man. Franck has become an artist of definite principles, whose genius is no longer tentative and uncultured, as in the first period, nor dreamy and tending towards new horizons, as in the second. He has now attained to perfect self-consciousness, knowing what he wants and possessed of a gift which, thanks to traditional atavism, combined with reflection and experience, is now capable of daring all things and building masterpieces both simply and solidly.

At this moment a final transformation takes place : Franck both *wishes* and *knows* how to compose. The hesitations of youth and the almost cloistral calm of his maturity are left behind ! As his pupil Ropartz * has remarked, it seemed as though he had "reposed a certain number of years in order to acquire the necessary strength to sustain this new career which opened out before him just as

* *Revue Internationale de Musique*, December 1890.

he had reached the age of fifty, like a dazzling path leading to new joy and radiance, towards which he pressed onwards, sure of himself and filled with fervent faith and youthful enthusiasm."

He now *knows* how to work out his numerous inspirations and *wills* to create. And his creations become radiant with vitality and brimming with beauty.

He does not intend to be a stranger to any form of his art, symphony, vocal music, chamber music, even lyric drama—he attacks them all in turn; there is not one realm in the universe of music that he fails to explore. And in the course of the conquest of this vast and new world he makes many rich discoveries, and effects the logical and inspired renascence of traditional forms.

I think I have already said enough as to what constitutes the originality of Franck's classical spirit, and need hardly return to it here; besides, it is only necessary to read through the works of his later years in order to realise it. I will not weary the reader with a dry and futile analysis of all the remarkable compositions which remain as the monument of his third style, but will confine my attention to the chief examples, reserving to myself the right to devote a more detailed study to the three immortal masterpieces—the *Quartet* in D major, the *Chorales* of 1890, and *The Beatitudes*.

It is with regret that I must only make bare mention of the fascinating *Eolides* and the *Three Pieces for Organ*, written expressly for the inauguration of the colossal organ at the Trocadéro during the exhibition of 1878, a collection which contains the *Cantabile* in B major, with its suave and devotional theme which will ever remain the typical prayer of an artist who was also a true Christian. Twice the prayer is heard; and here again we cannot fail to admire the wonderful canon which, moving with unbroken ease, forms the adornment of the melody, written by the master on purpose to display the warm, expressive quality of the new clarinet stop, recently discovered by Cavaillé-Coll.

Nor must I linger over the triumphal *Quintet* in F minor, the first chamber work which had appeared since the *Trios* in 1841, played at a concert of the Société Nationale, January 17, 1880, Saint-Saëns being at the piano, assisted by MM. Marsick, Rémy, Van Wœfelghem, and Loys; nor yet over *Rebecca* and *Le Chasseur Maudit*, first performed at the Société Nationale, on March 31, 1883. I must, however, call attention to one rather curious development which I pointed out in speaking of the works of Franck's first period : I mean his return to the composition of piano pieces, a style which he had completely neglected for nearly forty years.

For some time past composers had ceased to

write serious works for the pianoforte. After the avalanche of fantasias and the plethora of concertos which filled the first half of the nineteenth century, it seemed as though this instrument, which had been the inheritor of all the masterpieces of Bach, Haydn, and Mozart, and had acquired with Beethoven its true patent of nobility—was now destined, artistically speaking, to a sterile decadence. Although the great specialists of the piano had added to its technique some new and ingenious details ; although, to express the poetry of his soul in inspired trifles, Schumann had invented a style of writing for this instrument more orchestral than his orchestration itself, which blossomed forth in fascinating and intimate sonorities ; although Liszt had swept away at one stroke all the scaffolding of classic " pianism," enriched the instrument by means of combinations hitherto unsuspected, and given a decisive impulse to virtuosity—as yet no musician had added any fresh *artistic* material to the monument which Beethoven had left us. In short, though the technique of the piano and the style of writing for it had become transcendent, the music intended for the instrument *alone* had certainly degenerated ; and every form which does not progress ends by becoming atrophied and dying out.

The important movement started in France by the Société Nationale de Musique had only brought forth a very few interesting pieces for piano solo, its activity being chiefly directed to encouraging orchestral or chamber music. César Franck, struck by the lack of serious works in this style, set to work with a youthful fervour which belied his sixty years to try if he could not adapt the old æsthetic forms to the new technique of the piano, a problem which could only be solved by some considerable modifications in the externals of these forms.

It was in the spring of 1884 that he first spoke to us of this wish, and from that moment until 1887 his eyes dwelt perpetually upon the ivory of the keyboard.

He began by a piece for piano and orchestra, a kind of symphonic poem based upon an Oriental subject from Victor Hugo's *Les Djinns*, in which the pianist is treated as one of the *executants*, not as the soloist of a concerto, as custom had hitherto demanded. This work, which is not, properly speaking, a musical adaptation of Hugo's poetical "lozenge," * and is not even very closely connected with the subject, was only a first attempt, which soon found completion in the admirable *Prelude, Chorale, and Fugue* for piano solo. In this composition all is new both as regards invention and workmanship. This work was destined to add

---

* The expression, which seems cryptic to those unacquainted with Hugo's poem, can be easily understood by reference to "Les Orientales," No. 28, p. 115. *Les Djinns* opens with short lines which gradually lengthen to a climax and die down again, with an effect on paper somewhat resembling this figure : ◇ —R. N.

interest to the programmes of the Société Nationale, under the auspices of which it was first brought out by Mme. Poitevin, January 24, 1885. Franck started with the intention of simply writing a prelude and fugue in the style of Bach, but he soon took up the idea of linking these two movements together by a Chorale, the melodic spirit of which should brood over the whole work. Thus it came about that he produced a work which was purely personal, but in which none of the constructive details were left to chance or improvisation ; on the contrary, the materials all serve, without exception, to contribute to the beauty and solidity of the structure.

The *Prelude* is modelled in the same form as the prelude of the classical suite. Its sole theme is first stated in the tonic, then in the dominant, and ends in the spirit of Beethoven with a phrase which gives to the theme a still more complete significance. The *Chorale*, in three parts, oscillating between E flat minor and C minor, displays two distinct elements : a superb and expressive phrase which foreshadows and prepares the way for the subject of the *Fugue*, and the *Chorale* proper, of which the three prophetic words—if we may so call them—roll forth in sonorous volutions, in a serene, religious majesty.

After an interlude which takes us from E flat minor to B minor—the principal key—the *Fugue* presents its successive expositions, after the development of which the figure and rhythm of the com-

plementary phrase of the *Prelude* returns once more.
The rhythm alone persists, and is used to accompany
a strenuous restatement of the theme of the *Chorale*.
Shortly afterwards the subject of the *Fugue* itself
enters in the tonic, so that the three chief elements
of the work are combined in a superb peroration.

When interpreting this dazzling conclusion, it is
evidently the subject of the *Fugue* that should be
brought out by the pianist, for it is the keynote,
the reason for the existence of the whole work. We
find it as early as the second page of the *Prelude* in
a rudimentary but quite recognisable form :

it grows more distinct in the initial phrase of what
I have called the first element of the *Chorale :*

finally, after its full exposition in the first entry of
the *Fugue :*

the peroration to which I have referred above recalls
the subject combined with the other elements :

From this moment it appears in its full significance, and enfolds us in its triumphant personality until the final peal which brings the work to a close.

Very different in construction is the *Prelude, Aria, and Finale*, dedicated to Mme. Bordes-Pène, and played by her for the first time at the concert of the Société Nationale, on May 12, 1888. This work does as much for the renovation of sonata-form as its predecessor does for the prelude and fugue.

Here the theme of the *Prelude* is a long phrase in four sections of extraordinarily sustained inspiration. It is repeated in the relative key about the middle of the piece, and reappears at the close in the tonic (E major), with slight modifications. We recognise the form of the *Andante* in the sonata.

The *Aria* is the twofold exposition of a simple, tranquil melody which modulates from A flat major to A flat minor, framed as it were between a short introduction and a conclusion which reappears in the *Finale*.

As regards this last movement, it has the appearance and essential anatomy of sonata-form, with this difference—that the principal tonality appears for the first time with the restatement of the second subject and continues without any change until the end. The joyous effect of the return to this key is all the more intense because it has been recaptured with difficulty by means of a wonderfully varied gradation of tonalities. After the traditional development of the themes, the *Aria* is heard again, calm amid its animated surroundings, and in the key of D flat major. Then, after the re-exposition of the themes is accomplished, the noble melody of the *Prelude* establishes itself forcibly amid the principal tonality, to conclude, in a series of expressive tone-gradations, with the elements of the *Aria*. Contrary to the preceding work, this one has no tintinnabulant peroration, but dies away softly as though the melody evaporated and vanished in thin air.

It is difficult to decide which of these two works is the more inspired, but we may assert with absolute confidence that both gave a revivifying impulse to the literature of the pianoforte, which seemed about to perish between the Scylla and Charybdis of virtuosity and emptiness.

Between these two typical renovations of the art of writing for the piano we must place the *Variations Symphoniques* for piano and orchestra,* the continuation, as I have observed, of that amplification of this form which Beethoven began with such a master-hand.

To this period of very active production belong also the completion of *The Beatitudes*, the composition of *Hulda*, and the *Sonata in A for Violin and*

* First performed at the Société Nationale de la Musique May 1, 1885, M. L. Diémer being at the piano.

Piano, dedicated to Eugène Ysaye, about which I should like to say a few words, for this sonata is one of the most striking examples of the application of a system of lofty variation to traditional forms.

The melodic basis of this masterpiece consists of three themes, of which the first—the germ of the work—is presented in the beginning as a rhythmic figure :

and dominates in various forms the whole organism of the work.

As to the two remaining themes :

and

they appear in succession as the work progresses, and attain their full development when it reaches its climax.

I need hardly say that the first of these organic germs quoted above is used as the theme of all the four movements of the work, and that in the last movement (a bold transformation of the old rondo-form) it gives birth to an admirable example of

VAN HOUT   JACOB   FRANCK   EUGENE ISAYE   CRICKBOOM   PAUL BRAND

THIS PHOTOGRAPH WAS TAKEN ON THE OCCASION OF A CONCERT GIVEN ON APRIL 22ND, 1890, AT TOURNAI, THE LAST IN WHICH CÉSAR FRANCK TOOK PART

melodic canon, such as hitherto Franck alone was capable of inventing.

From this moment cyclical form, the basis of modern symphonic art, was created and consecrated.

The majestic, plastic, and perfectly beautiful Symphony in D minor is constructed on the same method. I purposely use the word *method* for this reason : after having long described Franck as an empiricist and an improvisor—which is radically wrong—his enemies (of whom, in spite of his incomparable goodness, he made many) and his ignorant detractors suddenly changed their views and called him a musical mathematician, who subordinated inspiration and impulse to a conscientious manipulation of form. This, we may observe in passing, is a common reproach brought by the ignorant Philistine against the dreamer and the genius. Yet where can we point to a composer in the second half of the nineteenth century who could—and did—think as loftily as Franck, or who could have found in his fervent and enthusiastic heart such vast ideas as those which lie at the musical basis of the *Symphony*, the *Quartet*, and *The Beatitudes*?

It frequently happens in the history of art that a breath passing through the creative spirits of the day incites them, without any previous mutual understanding, to create works which are identical in form, if not in significance. It is easy to find examples of this kind of artistic telepathy between painters and writers, but the most striking instances are furnished by the musical art.

Without going back upon the period we are now considering, the years between 1884 and 1889 are remarkable for a curious return to pure symphonic form. Apart from the younger composers, and one or two unimportant representatives of the old school, three composers who had already made their mark —Lalo, Saint-Saëns, and Franck—produced true symphonies at this time, but widely different as regards external aspect and ideas.

Lalo's Symphony in G minor, which is on very classical lines, is remarkable for the fascination of its themes, and still more for charm and elegance of rhythm and harmony, distinctive qualities of the imaginative composer of " Le Roi d'Ys."

The C minor Symphony of Saint-Saëns, displaying undoubted talent, seems like a challenge to the traditional laws of tonal structure ; and although the composer sustains the combat with cleverness and eloquence, and in spite of the indisputable interest of the work—founded, like many others by this composer, upon a prose theme, the *Dies Iræ*—yet the final impression is that of doubt and sadness.

Franck's *Symphony*, on the contrary, is a continual ascent towards pure gladness and life-giving light, because its workmanship is solid, and its themes are manifestations of ideal beauty. What is there more joyous, more sanely vital, than the principal subject of the *Finale*, around which all the other themes in the work cluster and crystallise? while in the higher registers all is dominated by that motive which M. Ropartz has justly called " the theme of faith." *

This Symphony was really *bound to come* as the crown of the artistic work latent during the six years to which I have been alluding.†

Psyche is a work which I particularly cherish, because the master did me the honour of dedicating it to me, joining to my name the precious designation of "friend." It was first performed at the Société Nationale on March 10, 1888, and revived at the Colonne Concerts on February 23, 1890.

I have already spoken of the mystical significance of this work, which, in spite of its antique title, has nothing of the pagan spirit about it, and still less of

* J. Guy Ropartz, *Symphonies Modernes ;* extract from *Notations Artistiques.* Lemerre, 1891.

† We must in justice deal with the erroneous view of certain misinformed critics who have tried to pass off Franck's Symphony as an offshoot (they do not venture to say imitation, because the difference between the two works is so obvious) of Saint-Saëns' work in C minor. The question can be settled by bare facts. It is true that the Symphony, with organ, by Saint-Saëns was given for the first time in England in 1885, but it was not known or played in France until two years later (January 9, 1887, at the Conservatoire) ; now at this time Franck's Symphony was completely finished.

the Renaissance, but, on the contrary, is imbued with Christian grace and feeling, recalling the frescoes in the Arena of Padua or the *Fioretti* of St. Francis of Assisi. I wish, however, to call the attention of my readers to what M. Derepas says on the subject in the pamphlet previously mentioned ; for his opinion is the result of minute observations which, coming from a learned and perfectly unbiassed critic, cannot fail to interest all those who are endowed with artistic feeling.

"According to the old myth, Psyche, touched by love, but tempted by an indiscreet haste for knowledge, and yielding to curiosity, falls back upon herself, powerless to rise again, and deprived for ever of the direct vision of the world beyond. Franck did not hesitate to break away from pagan tradition. His poem ends in a more optimistic spirit. Psyche falls asleep, ignorant of all external sounds. The Zephyrs—her pure inspirations—bear her to the garden of Eros, the desired paradise. Her celestial spouse awaits her. But she imprudently wishes to pierce the mystery in which he has enveloped himself. The sublime vision disappears. Fallen again to earth, wandering and plaintive, Psyche breathes forth her woe. Eros forgives the legitimate ambition which he himself had inspired. Together they soar back to the light. It is the apotheosis ; the love which has no need for faith, because it sees and possesses. It is indeed a true Redemption.

"Even more than its libretto, the music of Psyche is quite modern and Christian in its inspiration. The choruses are developed in so pure and suave a polyphony, kept at so high a level in a region of shadowless radiance, that neither the chorus of angels in 'La Damnation de Faust' nor 'L'Enfance du Christ' evokes so clearly the idea of heaven.

"Eros and Psyche do not express themselves in words. Their emotions are interpreted by the orchestra, and for this reason : they are not personalities. Franck, forgetful of the mythical hero and heroine, makes them the symbols of the human Soul and of supreme Love. Pure music, without the association of words, is the most adequate medium of expression for these immaterial actualities, precisely because its notes convey no definite significance, nor its phrases a precise meaning. In this oratorio, therefore, there are no solos. The orchestra plays the most important part; it depicts Psyche's transports, regrets, and final happiness, and the invisible but fruitful action of Eros. At the most, the chorus, anonymous and impersonal, sing here and there in a few words the movements of the drama.

"It is obvious that the entire work is impregnated with a breath of Christian mysticism. The sorrow of the exile on earth partakes of the accent of

prayer. The exceedingly sustained harmony of the
strings, the lines traced by the violins, the episodes
allotted to the wind, never betray the least sign of
sensuous preoccupations, but only express the highest
desires of a heart penetrated by the Divine Spirit." *

This mystical tendency—but towards a charming
and holy mysticism—is still more accentuated in
The Procession (first heard at the Société Nationale,
April 27, 1889), in *La Vierge à la Crèche* ("The
Virgin at the Cradle"), an exquisite picture, recalling
the primitive Umbrian School, in which the sincere
charm of the music atones for the somewhat
namby-pamby character of the words. It is as
though some little Madonna by Bartolo di Fredi
had left a wall in San Gimignano to make music in
Paris.

Traces of this religious tenderness may be seen
also in most of the versicles for the *Magnificat*,
published after Franck's death under the commonplace title of *L'Organiste*, *59 Pièces pour Harmonium*.

Which of us has forgotten our master's delight
when, alternating with the choir, he improvised
upon his organ the versicles of the Hymn to the
Virgin with which the vesper service closes? Then
there was no need for preoccupation, as at the
morning service, when the melodic and tonal construction of an offertory or communion required to

* Gustave Derepas, *op. cit.*

be swiftly but seriously thought out. Gone the questioning look on his mouth, the momentary hesitation as his hands hovered over the registers. This *Magnificat* was one continual smile; a broad smile upon a radiant face; a smile which was full of confidence and knew nothing of death—in a word, the smile of our "Father" Franck.

He threw himself into the improvisation of these versicles like a child into a round-game, and when towards the close of his life a publisher who knew what he was about asked him to fix these fugitive impressions in a collection of a *hundred* pieces for harmonium, he jumped at the suggestion, and set to work with such ardour that he often wrote four or five of these trifles in one morning. The work was cut short by his death.

M. Gardey, priest of Saint-Clotilde, who had known him for twenty-five years, and who came at his request to administer the last sacrament to him, told us that on the occasion of one of his visits to the dying genius—to whom his presence probably recalled these Sunday improvisations—Franck turned to him, his worn features still lit up with some of the old joyousness, and said : "Ah! that *Magnificat !* How I loved it! What a number of versicles I have improvised to those beautiful words! I have written down some of them—sixty-three have just been sent to the publisher, but I do want to get up to a hundred. I shall go on with them as soon as I get better—or else," he added in a lower tone, "perhaps God will let me finish them—in His eternity to come."

I must now turn to Franck's two attempts at dramatic music. The first was *Hulda*, begun in 1882 and finished in 1885; the second *Ghisèle*, the finished sketch of which is signed and dated September 21, 1889.

It may appear surprising that I should use the word *attempt* in speaking of these works; but, in spite of their great musical value, which is indisputable and undisputed, they do not seem to me to represent in the sphere of dramatic music that progressive movement, that generous and renovating impulse, which we find in all the symphonic works of the master's third period.

Strange to say, Franck's operas are, to tell the truth, less dramatic than his oratorios.

I think this æsthetic inferiority may be attributed in a great measure to the flagrant commonplaceness of the poems which were offered to him, which in no way rose superior to the libretti of historic opera, then in a moribund condition; but we must also add—and this is no reproach—that Franck's genius did not tend to the theatrical.

He was never theatrical, in his life or in his works. How then could he have conceived music solely

intended to make an effect on the stage, and to catch
the ear of the public at any price, which was all that
his operatic books were fit for? He was too sincere
and too conscientious ever to have harboured the
mere thought of such an art. He contented himself, therefore, with writing beautiful music, without
seeking for any new dramatic expression which could
not have been suggested by the texts at his disposal.

At the same time he almost took the bit between
his teeth (forgive the trite expression) at one moment
while composing *Hulda*; but it is remarkable that it
was the ballet that carried him away from the first,
and that was still symphonic music.

He wrote this ballet without pause or break, at
the same time as a prologue, which does not appear
in the score as it now stands, having been replaced,
no one knows why, by an epilogue. One evening
in the autumn of 1882, when Henri Duparc and I
called to see him, he came to meet us, flushed and
very much excited, and fired off these words at us,
which can only be really appreciated by those who
knew " Father " Franck : " I think the ballet of
Hulda is a very good bit of work ; I am very pleased
with it. I have just been playing it over to myself,
and—*I even danced it !* "

Hulda was given for the first time at the theatre
at Monte Carlo in 1894.

As to *Ghisèle*, it was written still more rapidly,

having been begun in the autumn of 1888, and completed, as I have already stated, in September 1889.

This was a prolific year, in which Franck, sure of himself, could write in his eight weeks' holiday the last two acts of his opera and his sublime String Quartet! It almost appears as though he foresaw his end, and hastened to utter all the music that still remained within him.

At his death *Ghisèle* was completely sketched out as regards orchestration, the first act being quite finished in this respect, and the five disciples who had the honour to complete the instrumentation of the two remaining acts were all sufficiently familiar with the master's intimate thoughts, as well as with his method of externalising these ideas in his pencil sketches, to find the task an easy one.*

The first representation of *Ghisèle* took place also at Monte Carlo on April 5, 1896.

We now reach the last works, which form a superb crown to an edifice of genius. Although absolute beauty defies description, I wish as far as possible to analyse and disclose the cause of the sensations produced by the three masterpieces which I have held over from the beginning of this chapter.

---

* The five pupils were: Pierre de Bréville, Ernest Chausson, Arthur Coquard, Vincent d'Indy, and Samuel Rousseau.

These sensations cannot be reproduced here, and my readers must forgive the impotence of my pen in describing them, showing some indulgence to a musician who is obliged to speak of his art in a language which is not that of the art itself. I shall endeavour to make my descriptions accessible to those who, knowing nothing of the musician's craft, love music and are sensible to beauty.

VII

THE QUARTET IN D MAJOR

THE form of composition known as the string quartet must be a work of maturity, if it is to have any real artistic significance.

Do not let it be supposed that I have any intention of laying down a dogmatic law. Heaven forbid ! The assertion, however, is proved by experience and corroborated by historical observation.

Even among musicians of genius there is no example of a really *good* string quartet which dates from a youthful period. Mozart's finest quartets date from 1789–90, when the composer was thirty-three—almost the equivalent of old age in this particular instance.

Beethoven waited until he was thirty before he ventured to handle this form of composition, having refused at twenty-seven the tempting offers made to him by Count Appony ; and it was not until nine years later, with the seventh quartet, in F, that he began to realise all that this form was capable of becoming. The first ten or eleven of his works in this sphere are merely essays, and the era of the true Beethoven quartet—of those which created a new art of music with the help of four instruments—only dates from 1822, when the musician was in his fifty-third year.

Edvard Grieg, in a sensational article upon his own early studies, written for an American paper,* relates that on his entrance to the Leipzig Conservatoire, Reinecke, as might be expected from a worthy German pedagogue, directed him to write a string quartet. The work was bad, as the composer himself frankly owns, but the results of this early educational mistake remained with Grieg, who, while he was a charming improvisor of more or less national songs, was no symphonist, and never succeeded in becoming one.

But, it may be objected, those who can write for orchestra must *a fortiori* be able to compose a quartet. This opinion is quite erroneous, and could only proceed from persons of superficial judgment.

There is scarcely any connection between the two methods of realising an idea by means of the string quartet of the orchestra and realising it in the form

* Edv. Grieg, "My First Success," *The Independent*, New York, 1905.

of chamber music. The basis, the form, the style of writing are in the latter case almost the opposite to what they would be in an orchestral symphony. Thus it comes about that *youthful* quartets—those written too early in life—though they may present certain seductive and ear-tickling qualities, soon grow old and perish for lack of solidity of structure.

It would be easy to explain the reasons for this, but I should be stepping aside from my subject, for this volume is not intended as a treatise on musical composition. I will merely emphasise the fact that the string quartet is the most difficult of all forms to treat worthily, and that in order to attain the variety in unity which it essentially demands, ripeness of intellect and talent, together with sureness of touch, are indispensable qualities.

It was during his fifty-sixth year that César Franck first ventured to think of composing a string quartet; even then, in 1888, when we used to see with astonishment his piano littered with the scores of quartets by Beethoven, Schubert, and Brahms, he did not get beyond the contemplation of the idea. The first actual sketches date only from the spring of 1889.

The first movement, the dominating idea, cost him infinite trouble. Frequently he would start afresh, rubbing out with a nervous hand all that he had believed to be permanent the day before. He built up a good third of the opening section upon a melodic idea, of which he afterwards modified almost the whole elemental structure. He did not hesitate even then to cut out what was already written in clear copy, and to begin again according to a second version, which in its turn failed to satisfy him, and was destroyed and replaced by a third and last scheme.

By way of proof, and for the edification of young writers who believe every phrase that comes from their pens to be immutable, I will reproduce here the three versions of this musical thought which plays so important a part in the development of the work.

In the same way Beethoven made five attempts before he definitely established the theme of the *Finale* of the pianoforte sonata Op. 53 ; and yet it seems to flow direct from the fountain of his inspiration.

Franck had no reason to repent the laborious conception of his first movement, for it was perhaps thanks to his hesitations and the retracing of his footsteps that he at last succeeded in finding the special form which fitted this masterpiece.

1re
Version

2me

Version

Version
définitive

This first movement is, indeed, the most wonderful piece of instrumental music which has been constructed since the last of Beethoven's quartets. Its form, which is essentially new and original, consists of *two* musical ideas, each living its own life and possessing its own complete organism, which interpenetrate without becoming merged in each other, thanks to the perfect ordering of their various elements and divisions.

Like the *Quintet* in F minor, the *Symphony* and the *Violin Sonata*, the *Quartet* is constructed upon a germinative idea which becomes the expressive basis of the entire musical cycle ; but no other work of Franck's— nor, indeed, of any of his predecessors—equals in daring but harmonious beauty this typical example of chamber music, which is unique not only in the worth and loftiness of its ideas, but in the perfection and novelty of its structure, which is highly original.

At the risk of being too technical, and consequently rather wearisome to some of my readers, I shall—for the sake of a few others—attempt to explain the union of these two elements of the quartet in one organic whole; and as I can find no suitable term by which to qualify these two parts of a whole, I will simply call them by the names generally applied to them in the *ensemble* of the first movement; that is to say, one is constructed in *lied*-form and the other in *sonata*-form.

The germinative theme of the cycle forms in itself alone the slow exposition of the *lied*: (Theme X.)

a complete exposition in the key of D major. To this succeeds, in an *Allegro*, the exposition of the *Sonata*, with its two subjects, the first in D minor : (Theme A)

the second in F major, in the classical style : (Theme B)

these two ideas linked together by a melodic figure : (Motive C)

which afterwards plays an important part in the *Finale*.

The exposition of the *Sonata* ends in F, the relative, and with the same figures as those of the *lied*.

Here, instead of the classical development of the sonata, the *lied* reappears in F minor, but treated fugally and with such continuity as to give it the importance of a middle section—an *andante :*

an admirable and mysterious meditation which unfolds gradually like the oncoming of the twilight, falling in more and more sombre tints.

Then the *Allegro* takes up the discourse once more, and shaking off the nocturnal veil which enwrapped the *lied*, compels the music, in an ascending development, to mount again towards the regions of light. But without success. In its restatement the *Allegro* only succeeds here and there in lifting the sable scarf, and it needs the calm and tender close of the victorious *lied* to bring us back, with the return of the principal key, to the long-awaited brightness.

In order to make my meaning clearer, let me add on the following page a diagram of the scheme, which it is difficult to explain in words. It will be easier to grasp the plan of this wonderful work if we refer to the themes already quoted, which I have indicated by letters, as in the demonstration of a mathematical problem.

But, as should always be the case with fine works

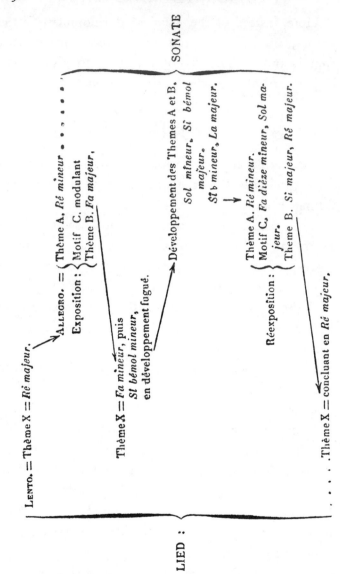

SONATE

Lento. = Thème X = Ré majeur.

Allegro. = ⎰ Thème A, Ré mineur • • • • • •
Exposition : ⎱ Motif C. modulant
            Thème B. Fa majeur,

Thème X = Fa mineur, puis
        Si bémol mineur,
en développement fugué.

Développement des Thèmes A et B.
        Sol mineur, Si bémol
                majeur,
        Si b mineur, La majeur.

Réexposition : ⎰ Thème A. Ré mineur.
              Motif C, Fa dièze mineur, Sol ma-
                jeur.
              Thème B. Si majeur, Ré majeur.

. . . . Thème X = concluant en Ré majeur.

LIED :

of art, the hearer scarcely suspects the exceptional and admirable structure of this masterpiece, of which he is made sensible by the feeling that he is face to face with something powerful and great, while at the same time he is carried away by the penetrating charm of the themes.

The *Scherzo* in F sharp minor, a frolic, " a round danced by sylphs in a moonless landscape," as it would have been described during the romantic period, was composed, or at least written, in ten days.   The sketch, which has scarcely any erasures, bears the date of November 9 ; whereas at the end of the first movement is recorded in large, sprawling letters, *October 29th, 1889*, followed by a note as to the duration of the movement : " 17 minutes."

As to the third movement, the *Larghetto* in B major—a favourite key of the composer's—it is also a model of purity, grandeur, and melodic sincerity.   I do not think since Beethoven wrote the slow movements of his later quartets that it would be possible to find in all musical literature a phrase so elevated and so perfectly beautiful in thought, in proportion, and in utterance as this long prayer.

For this, too, he sought long ere he found it. To us, his old pupils, he made no secret of his hopes and disappointments, his constant efforts in this respect.   With what joy he called to me from the other end of his sitting-room, when I went to

see him one day : " I have got it at last ! It is
a beautiful phrase ; you must see for yourself ! "
Without loss of time he hastened to the piano to
make me share in his happiness.

Ah, my master, in what hidden fold of your
" seraphic soul " (as our fellow pupil Alexis de
Castillon used to say) did you find the germ that
afterwards flowered and bore such fruit, and now
rises up, a glorious, full-grown tree, to the honour
of musical art ?

The *Finale* is well worth studying, although it is
not so spontaneous in structure as the first movement. It is in sonata-form, and opens with an
introduction in which the hearer will recognise in
succession the themes of the earlier movements ; a
familiar method of procedure, but one which is
rarely well carried out.

The first sketch for this introduction is rather
curious, at least as regards its conciseness, the
literary indication blending with the musical touch.
After having noted the intermediary working out
of the *Finale* (what the Germans call *Durch-
führung*) :

and having distinguished this quotation by the word
" Commencement," Franck writes with emphasis :

" A *new phrase* is needed here; see the Quartet in
E flat." * Then follows this indication : *at the
end—*

which proves that the sketches of the *Finale* were
thrown off before the composition of the *Scherzo*,
for which the above theme, put into ternary rhythm,
served as the theme of the *Trio*.†

Immediately afterwards—occupying three staves
—comes this observation : " In the middle of the
second section, or towards the close, or else before
the return of the beginning of the *Finale*, bring in a
reminiscence of the *Andante*." This is followed by
the music containing this reminiscence. Finally
we arrive at a whole series of themes, all marked
by notes of interrogation, among which appears the
one which he finally fixed upon for the initial
subject of the last movement. The study of these
two pages is instructive for all who wish to be

* Beethoven, Op. 127.

† Franck gave these sketches for the quartet to his pupil, our
dear and deeply lamented comrade Ernest Chausson. Mme.
Chausson has kindly allowed me to reproduce some fragments
from them.

enlightened as to the methods of composition adopted by a great musician ; methods which we find employed almost identically in Beethoven's sketch-books.

To return to the *Finale* of the Quartet. It offers this remarkable feature, that its two leading ideas emanate, as it were, from phrases or figures already employed in the first movement; but they are here presented in a new spirit and under quite different aspects.

In the figure below we shall easily recognise the germinative phrase of the *lied* (see Theme X.) :

given out by the viola as the first subject of the movement. As to the second subject, consisting of three phrases, like Beethoven's second themes, it derives its principal element—contained in its first section—

from the subjoined motive (C) in the first *Allegro* :

The two other phrases of the second subject :

and

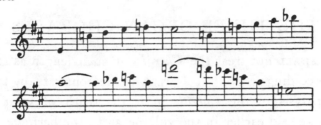

are peculiar to the *Finale*, although in the first we
may trace certain affinities of melodic outline with
the first movement.

The development displays a wonderful variety of
tonal colour. Passing from C sharp major (D flat)
to F sharp and D sharp (E flat), we rest for a
moment in B flat major, an intermediate key, and
D minor and major ; after which the music goes its
way until we reach the recapitulation, which follows
classical lines as far as the final development.   In
the middle of this, however, the persistent rhythm
of the *Scherzo* ends by recalling the radiant melody
of the *Larghetto*, which now appears in augmentation,
and brings this magnificent work to a close in a
spirit of almost religious solemnity.

Truly this *Quartet* is a work of rare beauty.

VIII

THE THREE ORGAN CHORALES *

I SHALL not treat the *Chorales* at such length as the preceding work, but I want to demonstrate by the analysis of the *Chorale* in E the truth of what I have said earlier in the volume as to the heritage of the great *Beethoven Variation,* which Franck alone seems to have cherished and endowed with added lustre.

In the present day, when every one has had a chance of hearing Bach's Passions and Cantatas, we cannot fail to know—if we have listened to them with attention—what constitutes the theme of a Chorale : the exposition of a series of short musical periods, separated by intervals of silence, the sequence of which forms a complete melodic phrase. This form, the outcome of Gregorian music, in which it blossomed out into free rhythms, became at the time of the so-called Renaissance the typical, collec-

---

* Franck dedicated these three chorales to MM. Al. Guilemant, Th. Dubois, and E. Gigout. It is by mistake that other names appear on the published edition.

tive choral music of the Protestant Reformation. But how greatly it lost in æsthetic value by its restriction within harmonic formulæ, instead of the free, expansive, Gregorian melody !

The Chorale, which after a short time came to be merely a song, was saved as regards its musical form by J. S. Bach, who, recapturing and raising to the height of his own genius the methods of the Catholic organists, created a new kind of Chorale Variation for the organ, a discovery which should have borne fruit, but by which, apparently, only Beethoven and Franck knew how to profit.

Franck's first *Organ Chorale* in E major offers one peculiarity—that the theme proper is first stated as an accessory part of a whole, which is equally in the form of a chorale, to which it serves merely as a conclusion (or in technical terms as a *Coda*).

The exposition of the work is therefore a *lied* in seven modulating periods, of which the sixth brings back and determines the key of E major, and it is completed by a seventh which seems to be super-added, but gradually takes its place as the dominating personality and suppresses all the others.

In order that my readers may follow this analysis by help of the music itself, I quote the opening notes of these seven periods :

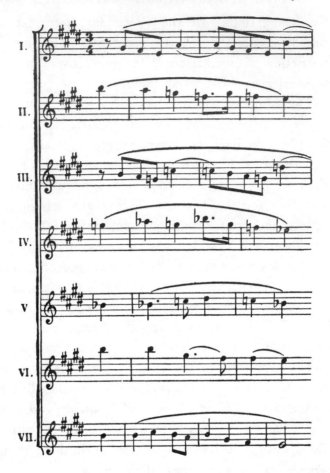

This fine exposition is succeeded by the First Variation, in which the entire phrase we have just heard is reproduced in a fragmentary way; that is to say, the periods II., IV., and VI. are omitted, and only those represented by the odd numbers are treated;

while the seventh already asserts itself in a way that marks it as more important than a mere *Coda*.

The Second Variation is rather a harmonic emanation (after Beethoven) than a commentary on the theme. Nevertheless it develops Nos. I. and IV. very clearly, although before long the seventh period alone carries on the whole musical discourse. Then the Third Variation takes possession of No. VII. and drags it with difficulty from the darkness in which the other periods have held it back, so that gradually it rises towards that final outburst in which, stated by the full power of the organ, it triumphs over all its companions in a joyful peroration in the key which has been reconquered at last.

This triumph "Father" Franck tried to explain to us in words which we could not grasp, because we did not know the work at that time : "You will see the *real* chorale," he used to say. "It is not the *Chorale* ; it is something that *grows out of the work*."

The two other *Chorales*, in B and A, are also conceived in the *great variation* form, and are equally fine. But to analyse them here would be to abuse my reader's patience, and the first one suffices to show how Franck assimilated (I do not say *imitated*) the principle of amplification which strikes us so greatly in all the later works of the composer of the Ninth Symphony.

IX

THE BEATITUDES

How singular has been the destiny of that style of composition called *Oratorio*, and how well worth a special study, for it constitutes one of the most curious examples of transformism in the whole history of the art.

Starting as a kind of mystical opera, oratorio soon became purely lyric, and then approximated to the symphonic form by adopting the style of the Cantata. But in our modern days, in this agitated period when all is provisionary, when faith, subjected to the assaults of disbelief, can no longer find its natural expression in art, musical oratorio has been imperceptibly led to replace and continue a literary form that was completely discarded : the Epic.

The epic, that poetic monument which we only approach with a kind of superstitious awe, because its manifestations, easily enumerated, have only occurred at long intervals in history, which we meet with only in ages of transition and under peculiar conditions, remained for long something which marked the passage from an established way of life to a new artistic and social state.

To the purely mystic and theocratic influences which have always sheltered the cradle of all young nations and civilisations, there invariably succeeds an era of strife, heroic in ancient times, chivalric in the Middle Ages, which precedes the period when the human being, even his physical personality, becomes the sole objective of the social movement, until the beginning of a new cycle which reproduces the order of those which have gone before.

It is, therefore, amid the period of agitation, of titanic wars, of internal strife, of sublime deeds and monstrous crimes that this mysterious lotus-flower of literature—the epic poem—invariably flourishes.

Such are the Homeric epics, fixing the language and mythology of Greece on the threshold of its civilisation ; such is the "Æneid," a lily which grew upon the very boundary-line which separated the heathen world at its most advanced stage of scepticism from that impulse of fervent faith whereon was grafted all Christian civilisation ; such, also, is the Comedy to which the epithet Divine has been so justly linked, which, originating amid the increasing struggles that rent all Italy, was nevertheless a work of pacification, wherein are gathered and concentrated all the learning of its day, all the exuberant faiths of which the Crusades were the generous outcome.

When the epic attempts to blossom outside its own environment or at unfavourable moments it loses a part of its meaning. It may be a skilfully versified poem, having a semblance of grandeur, like " Pharsalus," * " Paradise Lost," or "The Messiah," † but it remains all the same a work of artificial culture, and is not the long-awaited, needed, and universal manifestation.

In our day the human soul is too restless, too tossed and driven in every sense, to be equal to the *literary* creation of a work of simple faith such as the epic ought to be. The vague chant of rhythmic verse, be it in assonance or even in rhyme, no longer suffices to awaken the interest of the nations and bear to all men the poet's lofty message. Another element is now needed to act as intellectual inter-preter—an element endowed with a mysterious and half-divine influence—an element which is still young, which, by reason of its expressive nature, can adapt itself to that craving for dreams and ideals which will always exist in the depths of the human heart, in spite of all efforts on the part of the apostles of materialism to uproot it.

This vitalising element is music.

The nineteenth century has witnessed, from Beetho-ven to Franck, passing through Schumann, Berlioz, and Wagner, the birth of a great number of works,

* By Lucan.   † By Klopstock.

sacred and secular, which are nothing more or less than musical epics.

Such is the *Missa Solemnis,* in which the composer of the nine symphonies relates the life of Christ, the sublimity of His doctrine, and the thirst for fraternal peace which is the dream of the modern spirit. Epics, incomplete perhaps, but epical in their contents, are the " Faust " in which Schumann paraphrases Goethe's colossal poem, and the " Damnation " wherein Berlioz strives to assimilate this same masterpiece in the French spirit. An epic, too, is the Tetralogy in which Wagner has re-created, to the greater glory of music, the myths and symbols of Northern beliefs, as Homer before him condensed the Mediterranean legends. Finally the epic of *The Beatitudes,* in which " Father " Franck recounts, almost with *naïveté,* the beneficent action upon human destiny of a God Who is all love.

In this musical poem all the conditions needful in classic ages for the constitution of an epic are fulfilled : unity, sublimity, plenitude and interest of subject, the fitness of the poet and the environment, the former creating a work of faith in an age undermined by unbelief, himself firmly convinced of all that he relates, and dominating even sceptics by his musical eloquence, vaguer, but more universally captivating than a versified poem. *The Beatitudes,* then, are the long-expected work of the close of the nineteenth century, the masterpiece which, in spite of a few inevitable weaknesses (*aliquando bonus dormitat Homerus*), will remain a superb temple, solidly based upon the traditional foundations alike of faith and music, and rising above the agitations of this world like a fervent prayer ascending to Heaven.

As is almost invariably the case with all great monuments of art, the appearance of *The Beatitudes* was preceded by a very long period of preparation in the life of its creator.　As in the *Vita Nuova* we find some foreshadowings of the *Divine Comedy*, so we shall recognise with astonishment the sketch of the theme which afterwards served as the hallmark of the Ninth Symphony in a simple *lied* which Beethoven jotted down in 1804.

The Beatitudes had always existed, for they were the work of Franck's *whole evolution*.

From his early youth, from the moment when he felt that he was no longer a virtuoso, but a creative musician, he began to think of a musical setting of that beautiful poem of ideas—the Sermon on the Mount.　How could this Christian, in his strong and simple faith, fail to be attracted by this promise of future bliss?　How could this Christ, moving amid the multitude and shedding among them words of justice and peace, be for Franck anything but the musical incarnation of a God of Love, healing with a gesture the sufferings of humanity?

Franck loved this text, and constantly re-read it. A copy of the Holy Gospels which he had won as a prize at the end of a school year is preserved in his family, and the page containing in eight paragraphs the Divine Sermon shows traces of being worn by frequent use; moreover, in the margin beside each of Christ's sayings there are nail-marks—those nail-marks which we, his pupils, knew so well, because when he had no pencil within reach he used to underline in this way such passages in our exercises that he wished to praise or blame.

A very old piece for the organ, dating from his start as an organist, the manuscript of which has been lost, bore these words : " The Sermon on the Mount "; the same title reappeared on a *Symphony for Orchestra*, in the style of Liszt's symphonic poems, which also dates from an early period and has not been published.*

To transcribe this Divine poem in a musical paraphrase worthy of the subject was the master's constant thought ; but for this he required a versified text.

Having too little confidence in his literary training,

* M. Georges C. Franck possesses the manuscript of this symphony, together with a number of unpublished studies and pieces by his father.

he did not venture to undertake the work himself,
and (happily !) the librettists of the hour did not
care to lose valuable time in supplying this obscure
organist with a book for which the pecuniary return
was extremely doubtful.

Franck, who was not the shy and unapproachable
ascetic described by certain ignorant critics, very
gladly accepted friendly invitations to dine or spend
the evening out; he enjoyed going to a few con-
genial houses as a relaxation after the hard work of
the day, and was often to be met in the family circle
of M. Denis, then professor at the Lycée Saint-
Louis. Struck by the enthusiasm with which his
organist friend discussed in intimate conversation
the Sermon on the Mount, the plan of which was
growing more clearly in his mind, needing only a
text in order to become music, M. Denis endeavoured
to find a literary collaborator for Franck, and discovered her in the person of Mme. Colomb, the wife
of one of the professors at the Lycée of Versailles.

Mme. Colomb had a great facility for versification, and had already published a few poems which
had gained one of the annual prizes offered by the
Institute.

The musician, in several interviews, explained to
her the outline of the poem as he conceived it,
and as he had pondered it for many years, and
on this basis Mme. Colomb supplied him with

verses which, without being remarkable as poetry, do not hamper the music, and are certainly preferable to anything he might have got in this style from a professional librettist.

At last the master was provided with the text so long and ardently desired. He set to work at once, but everything did not run quite smoothly. He retouched, and retouched again, and it seemed as though, at first, the composer was not very sure what musical style to employ, but was groping his way ; and these tentative movements are still noticeable, especially in the first part of the work.

The Prologue, however, came to him fairly easily, and in the autumn of 1870 the first two *Beatitudes* were sketched out musically. During the winter of 1871, being still too much under the dominion of the agony then weighing on the heart of the whole French nation, and being unable to give his mind to the creation of anything new, he devoted his spare hours to the orchestration of these first sections, completing them in the midst of the bombardment of Paris. After the break caused by the composition of *Redemption*, he took up the work again and wrote the third part (" Blessed are they that mourn "), which seems to have given the work a definite tendency as regards style ; then came the sublime hymn to Justice, assigned to tenor solo, after which there were no further interruptions, and the work

was finished in the autumn of 1879. He spent
ten years upon the construction of this monumental
work.

It was not until long after its completion that the
first performance of the masterpiece by the Association Artistique took place, under the conductorship
of Edouard Colonne. This was in the winter of 1891,
a year after the master's death, and, as I have already
said, this performance assumed all the importance of
a revelation in the eyes of artists and of the public.

Shortly afterwards the second performance of *The
Beatitudes* was given at Liège, the composer's native
town, under the direction of Théodore Radoux, on
April 1, 1894. In the same year the work was performed twice at Utrecht, on June 18 and December 18 ; and in the course of the following year the
distinguished conductor Viotta * gave it in the huge
hall of the Concertgebouw, Amsterdam, with a chorus
of over six hundred voices.

Meanwhile the Société des Concerts of the Paris
Conservatoire had only ventured to give (and how
timidly !) two fragments from the work, and it was
not until 1904 that *The Beatitudes* figured in its
entirety—at two successive concerts—on these programmes. By that time the work no longer stood
in need of this tardy consecration in order to acquire
fame.

* Director of the Conservatoire at The Hague.

The poem falls naturally into eight sections, preceded by a prologue—or, perhaps, in order to follow out its conformity with the traditional epic, I ought to say into eight *cantos*. Each of these forms is itself a short poem, containing antithetically a double picture : first an exposition, sorrowful or indignant, of the vices and evils which reign on earth ; then the celestial affirmation of the expiation of these vices and the healing of these evils ; finally, either interpolated between the two, or in the form of a conclusion, the voice of Christ is heard proclaiming in a few words the beatitude which awaits those who are healed and sanctified. Each section of the poem, therefore, actually resembles a triptych in the most literal sense, in which two wings face and complete each other by contrast, while the central panel is occupied by the radiant figure of Christ, always the same, yet always different by reason of His varied attitudes.

This conception, so harmonious in the correspondence and perfect balance of its constituent parts, emanated from Franck himself ; a fact which I cannot insist upon too often, for it is remarkable at a time when no musician thought of troubling himself about the disposition and realisation of his subject, leaving it all to his librettist.

What, indeed, could be more characteristically "Franckian" than this work in which, apart from the *rôle* which this incomparable musician reserved to himself, we find a kind of pictorial atavism, instinctively borrowing from his ancestors, artistic or lineal, their wonderful comprehension of the triptych, together with the genius of the architect uniting all these pictures into a solid and powerful structure, and, finally, the faith of the Christian reproducing with the perfect simplicity of the primitive believers the figure of God made Man?

If I dwell upon the Christ of *The Beatitudes*, it is because the master has given in his work an interpretation of the Divine Personality such as had never before been contemplated in the whole history of music. Too timid, or too respectful, the great musicians of the polyphonic period, and that which followed, did not venture to represent the Son of God speaking and appearing as a real personage. If the Heavenly Gardener meets the Magdalen* His words are assigned, as in the dramatic madrigals, to collective interpretation. Later on the Christ appears occasionally in Cantatas and Oratorios, but He almost invariably keeps the character of a rigid Protestantism. With Handel, with Bach more especially, He is the strong, terrible, and sublime God enthroned above the world, shedding upon humanity below words of peace or condemnation; but we never see Him stooping towards the humble

* Heinrich Schütz, *Dialogus per la Pascua.*

and the insignificant; nor do we find Him near us, living our life, suffering our pains and pitying our sorrows with the fatherly tenderness which we find in every page of the Gospels. Still later He passes with Berlioz into the phase of legendary illusion, although bearing as yet a certain poetic stamp. For others He remains just simply " the fine Nazarene," or perhaps something worse—a mere pretext for the writing of cavatinas and ariosos. Henceforward nothing is left of the Divine figure, and His musical presentment suffers terribly from this, and becomes conventional and sickly in its insipidity.

César Franck makes no attempt to run a wild-goose chase—if I may be pardoned the commonplace phrase. Such as he has learned to love and know Christ, such he presents Him to us in *The Beatitudes* out of the fulness of his simple, Christian heart. In doing this he had recourse, so we are assured, to Ernest Renan's "Life of Christ." If so, it was most assuredly to proclaim the contrary, for the inconsistent character of the man who desired to make himself God, as described by that vague genius, has actually nothing in common with the image of the God Who was made man for the comfort and salvation of humanity—the pure conception of this good and devout musician.

It is this figure of Christ, or rather the sound of His voice, that constitutes the unity of the work from the musical point of view, that forms the centre, the principal subject, around which are grouped the different elements of the poem. Some of these elements, judged by their importance, their complexity, and the lavish musical means employed, seem calculated to absorb more than their share of the hearer's attention; but every time the voice of Christ is heard, if only for a few bars, all the rest is effaced while this Divine figure comes to the front, touching us to the very depths of our souls. For Franck has succeeded in finding for his Christ a representative melody actually worthy of the Personality of whom it is the musical commentary.

This melody, so simple yet so striking that we can never forget it after its first appearance in the Prologue, only attains its fullest development in the last *Canto*, where it then becomes so sublimely inspired that, hearing it unfold itself like spiral clouds of incense rising beneath the vaulted roof of a cathedral, we seem actually to take part in the radiant ascension of the faithful to their celestial dwelling.

Since to attempt a detailed analysis of this musical epic would exceed the scope of this chapter without being of much use to the reader, I must limit myself by pointing out to such musicians as are ready and willing to study the score for themselves the

salient points and the hidden foundations of the
work.

The Prologue, assigned to tenor recitative, is
merely a simple representation by various instrumental *timbres* of the phrase which personifies Christ
the comforter and dispenser of charity; Christ is
foreshadowed, but does not yet express Himself in
words.

Here the motive is not affirmative, as it afterwards
becomes, but, on the contrary, it is mysteriously
hesitating in its expressive syncopations:

The first section, " Blessed are the poor in spirit, for
theirs is the kingdom of heaven," is obviously the
weakest part of the work. Although in its second
aspect, which varies the first, the chorus intended
to express the twofold sentiments of the pleasure-
seekers and the disillusioned begins to approach
more nearly to the true Franckian melody, it is in
reality nothing but an operatic chorus in the style
of Meyerbeer, aggravated by a vulgar *stretto*. But as
soon as this theatrical number has come to an end

the Voice of Christ is heard for the first time : a long melodic phrase, independent of the theme of Charity, which impresses us by its nobility, and is afterwards repeated and amplified by the celestial chorus.

It should be noted that this first Beatitude is constructed in precisely the same manner as the first part of *Redemption ;* the opening chorus is in A minor and has more than one point in common with that of *Redemption ;* moreover, just as in the last-named work, the entrance into the celestial regions is effected in the key of F sharp major, which, for Franck, always represented the light of Paradise.

I cannot remember which of his critics gave vent to the opinion that, skilled as this master was in the use of *canon,* he rarely had recourse to fugue. Without mentioning some of the organ pieces and the famous fugue for piano, *The Beatitudes* are a splendid refutation of this criticism. The second section of this oratorio (" Blessed are the meek : for they shall inherit the earth ") can only be regarded as a fugue, the exposition of which is perfectly regular, with its subject :

Le ciel est loin La terre est sombre Nul rayon n'y luit;

counter-subject, its successive entries of the parts,

and its classical development, until we come to the consolatory quintet in D, of which the fervent melody seems to descend from the heights above like an actual ray of hope; the choir, now subdued, mingles with the soloists and completes the impression by a chromatic passage of exquisite tenderness, after which the Voice of Christ, reciting the text of the Gospel itself, puts the finishing touch to this beautiful number.

The third part is the song of sorrow: "Blessed are they that mourn : for they shall be comforted." Above a kind of persistent knell, a theme is given out in F sharp minor, the principal subject of an *Andante* in five parts, sombre in mood, concentrated in its sadness, although, even then, somewhat theatrical in style. The sections which pair, enclosed between three repetitions of the theme, are devoted to the expression of particular sorrows : here we have the mother weeping for her child, the timid orphan, the husband robbed of the tenderness of the wife. Later we come to the slaves sighing for liberty (here again is an instance of fugue), followed by the thinkers and philosophers who tell of their doubts and vain researches in the identical theme of slavery previously heard in D minor, but now transposed into D major, as though Franck, moved by a kind of simple irony, had intended to link philosophy to servitude. But, after one last cry of anguish, comes a sudden change, a fresh modulation from F sharp minor to E flat major brings back the theme of Charity, and, for the first time, the Voice of Christ is heard singing this motive, no longer hesitant and broken as in the Prologue, but affirmative and sure, the manifestation of the love awaited by the unhappy sufferers :

Heureux ceux qui pleu-rent, Heureux ceux qui pleu-rent, Car ils se-ront con-so-lés

The melody, which was formerly sad, is now transformed, and, given out by the celestial choir, it assumes the character of a theme of consolation. Presently the mystic breeze which wafted to us the words of Christ dies away in the distance, and everything comes to an end in calm and serenity.

It is beautiful indeed.

In the fourth part (" Blessed are they which do hunger and thirst after Righteousness : for they shall be filled ") the master's genius is revealed absolutely and without blemish. Here there is only room for admiration.

To the orchestra is assigned the exposition of the

two principal ideas which form the basis of this
Beatitude, the element of desire :

and the element of confidence :

this melody, following an ascending line, is developed
in conjunction with the first, and ends by being
definitely established in the tonality of G major.
Then, upon the mediant of the key, but still in the
feeling of the opening B minor, a tenor voice proclaims in words that which the orchestra has just
suggested in sonority ; the phrase—a *true* melodic
phrase—extends, grows more fervid, and, kindling
to a paroxysm of enthusiasm, breaks forth, in the
predestined key of B major, into the theme of sup-
plication.   From this moment onwards desire is
appeased and the sense of confidence alone persists,
while the Voice of Christ, combined with this theme
of answered prayer, returns to ratify the old promise :
" Ask and it shall be given unto you," an outburst
which comes in the long-expected key of B major.

The fifth part (" Blessed are the merciful : for
they shall obtain mercy ") shows us, as in *Redemption*,

humanity overrun by crime and violence. Christ
has turned away his face from the impious world ;
and here Franck has recourse to a device which would
have found favour with the mystical sculptors of our
Gothic cathedrals, for he employs the theme of
Charity *by inversion*, which invests it with a strange
aspect of sorrow and suffering :

After the tenor has set forth the situation, a
chorus of the rebellious, mad for vengeance, breaks
out in a somewhat artificial and theatrical hubbub,
which is by no means improved by a *stretto* written
according to the conventions of opera during its
" Judaic " period. Were it not absolutely contrary
to Franck's character—for he is always sincere even
in his errors—we might be tempted to think that
this inferior chorus had been placed there inten-
tionally in order to enhance the beauties which
follow ; but such a suspicion of calculated effect
could never even have flitted through the master's
mind, and if he has only succeeded in expressing the
desire for vengeance by the use of commonplace
phrases, it is because this desire was a thing so

foreign to his nature that he could not assimilate it even in imagination and with the sole object of giving it expression in music. When the hubbub has subsided, calm reigns once more. The Voice of Christ is heard admonishing this fruitless hatred, and at the words " pardon your brethren " a ray of sunshine pierces the clouds ; the theme of Charity brings back the light together with the key of D major, the tonality in which the work closes, and the celestial chorus completes the paraphrase of this sunrise by a phrase of ineffable sweetness, allied to the angelic melodies in *Redemption*, but very superior from the artistic point of view.

The sixth *Beatitude* is that of purity : " Blessed are the pure in heart : for they shall see God." In this section Franck's lofty soul moves in its own element. Apart from a few short passages in which the interest somewhat slackens, I do not think any truly artistic spirit could fail to be stirred to continuous and increasing admiration by this *Beatitude*.

The Heathen and Jewish women mourn for their departed Gods in a tender lament in which the two themes combine and mingle easily, in spite of the double tonalities of B flat minor and D flat major ; a quartet of Pharisees, which is perhaps a trifle too emphatic and resembles somewhat in spirit Heinrich Schütz's dialogue between the Pharisee and the

Publican, starts a series of vain self-justifications, which are fortunately interrupted by a short recitative for the Angel of Death, summoning both the hypocrites and the truthful before the judgment-seat of God.

The gates of Heaven are thrown open, and in the scintillant brightness of the key of F sharp major a flight of angels is heard singing the adorable melody in which Franck's *purity of heart* found its fullest expression. The exquisite cadence with which this chorus ends :

Pour vous s'ou.vri . ra   le saint lieu

is nothing more than a development of the Charity motive, taken up at once by the Voice of Christ in the actual words of the Gospel. After a series of brief commentaries in which the vocal parts seem to be weaving such garlands of flowers as we see in representations of Paradise by Lippi and Fra Angelico, Christ proclaims the words of consolation once more, but this time in the definite tonality of D major, which is that of the final outburst of glory ; then, by the simple device of raising the A natural to A sharp, we are brought back to F sharp major, and the choir brings the song to a close in the full radiance of this key.

I think this monument of artistic purity can never fall into decay.   It will remain a marvel worthy of adoration.

It would have been difficult to keep at such altitudes ; consequently with the seventh *Beatitude* ("Blessed are the peacemakers : for they shall be called the children of God ") we descend to earth—and even a little lower, because a somewhat conventional Satan endeavours to drag us down to the Pit.

This personification of *ideal evil*—if it is permissible to link these terms—was a conception so alien to Franck's nature that he never succeeded in giving it adequate expression.   I can never forget his efforts to put on an awe-inspiring air, his frowns, the contortions of his mouth and the queer sounds of his voice, which caused us to smile rather than tremble, when he sang :

C'est moi l'esprit du mal   qui suis roi de la ter . re

Poor, dear master ! His good faith was unshaken, and he honestly believed himself for the moment to be " the spirit of evil "—he who had only lived and worked for *good !*   Incapable, therefore, of drawing upon himself for the expression of emotions which he never felt but superficially, he borrowed the style of the most inferior eclectics, and here, more than in the first and fifth sections, he falls back on Meyerbeer.

The *stretto*,

> A day of wrath and judgment dire,
> Our day at length appeareth,

would not be out of place in some new version of " Robert le Diable."

At length Christ appears on the scene, the Devil is cast down, and the Saviour's recitative brings to the listener a delicious sense of refreshment, due to the serenity of the key B flat major coming after all the raving and ranting in minor keys which preceded it. This suave colouring of B flat major reappears later on in a very happy way, in the beautiful quintet in D flat which concludes this section; it is definitely established at the words " Satan's myriads lurk " as the tonal antithesis of the C minor of the Prince of Darkness.

At this point I wish to call attention for the last time to what I have already maintained in several preceding pages of this book as to the heritage left us by Beethoven which, in his own day, Franck was almost the only one to gather up and render fruitful. In *The Beatitudes*, more perhaps than in any other of his works, he makes use of the means supplied by fugue and variation-form. The former is to be found in the second, and, in its fullest development, in the third section, without enumerating other less striking instances. As regards the highest variation-form, we meet it on every page of the work : in the theme of Charity under its various aspects ; in practically the whole of the first section ; in the angelic idealisation of a theme of human suffering like that which occurs in the third section. This system of variation comes directly from Beethoven's *last quartets*, and has nothing in common with the Wagnerian *leitmotiv*, which does not consist of a transformation, but of a thematic development that finds its true application in the drama, but would not be admissible in a work thought out almost symphonically, like Franck's music poem.

We have now reached the crown of the work. that eighth *Beatitude* which, summing up all the others, is also an exceptional landmark in the history of music. We might almost believe that " Father " Franck, foreseeing a time of persecution, and becoming himself like the *vates* of the old epics, intended this masterpiece as a healing balm to those who were to suffer for justice' sake, and wished to compel them to look above, where peace and truth reign for all eternity.

" Blessed are they which are persecuted for righteousness' sake : for theirs is the kingdom of heaven."

Satan has reappeared; the spirit of evil, arrogant but devoured with unrest, tries to prove to Christ the emptiness of Love's victory. Here he is admirable, for his personality becomes almost human. He is no longer the Satan of the theatre, clothed in conventional tinsels; he is man, whose pride has suffered through defeat, who spues forth his hatred before the throne of his conqueror. This feeling, which is no longer a generalisation or an abstraction, but an expressive impulse, has been interpreted by Franck in an outburst of superb defiance.

But He whom Satan defies disdains to reply; and it is the Just, persecuted but confident in Justice to come, whose voices are now heard singing that it is sweet to die while proclaiming the one and only Truth. The contrast between the key of E major in which this fine melody is sung and the sombre colouring employed for Satan's defiance is very striking.

The Spirit of Hatred now apostrophises these mortals who brave him, and condemns them to the most horrible torments; while the Just, calm in spite of his threats, invoke eternity with ever-increasing confidence. Satan, confounded, replies with fiercer insults, and the chorus raises a third invocation, somewhat anguished at first, but soon giving place to complete tranquillity, and a delicious modulation brings us back to E major, emphasising the return of unshaken faith.

All grows dark once more, but in the mild colouring of F minor, and the Virgin in a sublime arioso, worthy of those in Bach's " Passions," comes to symbolise in herself the spirit of Sacrifice. With the words of her Divine offering the key of F major becomes established for the first time in the score.

Satan becomes powerless, withdraws into outer darkness, and Christ, victorious, enthroned above the world, summons all the host of the righteous and the elect :

> O come, ye of my Father beloved,
> O come to me !

At this juncture the key of D major, which has often appeared episodically, now becomes definite, and seems to fall upon regenerated humanity like a new light, while the Divine Voice is heard at last singing the long-expected song of salvation won through Love. The theme of Charity, hitherto so often torn asunder in so many fragmentary phrases, now becomes a complete melody, and the orchestra takes it up more solemnly than before, while the celestial and terrestrial choirs sustain their long and serene Hosannas.

In the whole of this sublime peroration there is

not one poor bar, not a note out of place, not a single modulation which is not explicable and approved by the dramatic situation.

This is true art. The ages to come cannot tarnish its resplendent beauty.

In conclusion, *The Beatitudes* bears the impress which seals so superbly all the strongest and most enduring manifestations of genius ; it is the ascending progression of a harmonious whole. In spite of some defects, which, as a historian, I may have too scrupulously emphasised, this musical epic is undoubtedly the greatest work which has found a place in the development of the art for a very long time past. This is also the opinion of a critic whose good faith is beyond question : *

" This work," he says, " is not merely one of the most extensive that has been composed since Beethoven's time, but it appears to me to rise above all the other compositions of the present day. I might, perhaps, point to more perfect works, but I know of none of such lofty and sustained inspiration. Here we find a radiance of the sublime ; and, wonderful to relate, this is not due to any external aid, but simply to the power of a unique emotion—to religious effusion alone."

Truly our revered master has " done well," as Emmanuel Chabrier said above his half-closed

* René de Récy, *La Revue Bleue*, 1894.

grave, and none can doubt that the Spirit of Eternal Righteousness has admitted him in the new life to that Beatitude the glory of which he sang so worthily in this world.

THE TEACHER AND HIS
HUMAN WORK

I

" FATHER " FRANCK

To teach an art with fruitful results we must first understand our *craft*, then the *art*, and finally the *pupil* whom we have undertaken to initiate.

It seems a mere commonplace to say that a teacher should himself be well instructed both in his craft and in his art—two distinct branches of study, although too often confused—but, as a question of practice, this statement is not remarkable, for in Germany as well as in France (Italy is not to be considered from this point of view) in all the teaching institutions there are very few professors of composition who know how to teach their *art*, because—it must be confessed—they only understand and exercise it empirically.

In my time there were even some teachers of composition at the Paris Conservatoire who did not thoroughly understand their own *craft*, and were therefore totally incapable of imparting it to others.

As to the knowledge of an individual pupil, our entire system of instruction in France being based upon the false principle of reducing all intellects to one level, it is not surprising that our professors of art, acting in agreement with systems adopted elsewhere, are only employed in pouring into young minds that are sometimes widely differentiated the same identical and trivial material, never realising that the pabulum which is good, or at least harmless, for some may be hurtful to others, to whom it should be administered with a corrective or an explanation. Nor do they grasp the fact that precepts necessary to limited minds can become intolerable to students of higher capacity, and may lead to a dangerous or at least premature affranchisement.

It is unnecessary to dwell any further on Franck's skill in the exercise of his craft and on the mastery displayed in his art, but it is important to show clearly one most valuable quality of his teaching— that knowledge of the individual pupil which was wanting in almost all the other professors of composition of his time.

Was he himself aware that he possessed this particular faculty? It seems doubtful; and we might go on to say that Franck was an unconscious philosopher, who studied the psychology of his pupils in spite of himself (I will explain the reason of this later on), and understood how to give each of them the direction and the subject-matter best suited to his temperament. He excelled in his

THE MONUMENT TO CÉSAR FRANCK
Alfred Lenoir, sculptor

power to penetrate his pupils' thoughts and to take possession of them, while scrupulously respecting their individual aptitudes. This is the reason why all the musicians formed in his school have acquired a solid science of music, while in their works each has preserved a different and personal aspect.

The secret of this essentially wide education lies in the fact that Franck never taught by means of hard and fast rules or dry, ready-made theories, but that his whole teaching was inspired by something stronger than law—by love itself.

Franck loved his art, as we have seen, with a passionate and exclusive ardour, and for this particular reason he loved also the pupil who was to become the depository of this art which he revered above all else; this is why he knew instinctively how to touch the hearts of his pupils and attach them to himself once and for all.

For the entire generation that was so fortunate as to be brought up on his sane and solid principles, César Franck was not merely a far-seeing and lucid teacher, but a *father*—and I have no hesitation in using this word to characterise the man who gave birth to the French symphonic school, for we, his pupils, together with many artists who came in contact with him, were drawn instinctively by a unanimous, but independent, agreement to call him "Father" Franck.

While the ordinary run of academic teachers (and especially the professors at the Paris Conservatoire, where their energies are chiefly directed to the production of *premiers prix*) generally succeed in making their pupils rivals—who often end by being enemies —" Father " Franck only set himself to turn out artists truly worthy of this free and noble title ; such an atmosphere of love radiated from this pureminded man that his pupils not only cared for him as for a father, but they were attached to each other in and through him. During the fifteen years which have elapsed since his death his beneficent influence has continued, so that his disciples have kept up their intimacy without the smallest cloud appearing to darken their friendly relations.

But, besides all this, what an admirable professor of composition he was! How sincere and conscientious in examining the sketches we took him ! Merciless to all faults of construction, he knew how to put his finger on the mistake without a moment's hesitation ; and when in the course of his corrections he came to the passages which we ourselves considered doubtful, although we had been careful not to tell him so, his wide mouth would immediately become serious, his forehead would be puckered up, and his whole attitude expressed suffering. After having played through the unfortunate passage two or three times on the piano, he would raise his eyes

to us and let drop the fatal words : " I don't like
that ! " But when by chance in our first stammer-
ing musical utterances we hit upon some new
modulation logically brought about, or some attempt
at novelty of form which had a certain interest, he
would bend over us murmuring : " I like this, I like
this ! " He was as happy in giving us this sign of his
approbation as we were proud to have deserved it.

But let it not be supposed that it was vanity or
presumption that caused the master to deduce his
judgments from his own likes and dislikes. Nothing
could be further from his mind than the arrogant
assertions of the *art critic*, announcing sententiously,
after a first—and often an absent-minded—hearing,
that " this work is sublime, and that one a failure."
" Father " Franck never criticised in this free and easy
fashion ; he listened, re-read, argued for and against,
and only formed his opinion when, after attentive
self-examination, he felt sure he was in inward communion with the spirit of Beauty and could speak
in the name of Truth—not of relative, but of
absolute truth.

For—as we who live at the close of the nineteenth
century know only too well—Truth is never made
manifest through hatred, and the words *"I condemn,"*
monstrous and frequent though they be, always
remain powerless compared with " Father " Franck's
simple utterance : " *I like it.*"

" To love, to come out of ourselves, to leave our egotism aside by loving something very superior—almost unknown, perhaps—in which, however, we continue to believe, no matter what name we give it—here is the very basis and essence of a true system such as Plato recommended to the worshippers of the celestial Venus; such as Bossuet taught Christians to regard as the voice of moral perfection. It is the system of all great artists; it was that of César Franck. Through it he came practically into touch with all those masters who have best depicted the ascent of the soul towards God." *

I now want my readers to penetrate more deeply into this intuitive manner of teaching, and see how much it differed from the methods employed by the majority of professors in conservatoires and music schools.

The first condition which Franck imposed upon a pupil was not to work *much*, but to work *well;* or, more strictly speaking, not to bring him a great quantity of task-work, but only what had been very carefully prepared.

The student gained greatly by this system, for he acquired the habit, even from his preliminary studies, of neglecting nothing and of bringing up work that was more intelligent than mechanical. This is a

* G. Derepas, " César Franck."

thing which too many young people educated in
more or less official institutions cannot grasp.
Accustomed from their childhood to bring *tasks* to
their professors, they cannot conceive that, in Art,
such a thing is non-existent. There is no more
occasion for task-work in musical composition than
there is in painting or architecture; all that is done
in the way of art should not be of the nature of a
daily imposition, but the result of a struggle in
which the young artist has left something of his
heart, and for the expression of which he has called
into play all his intellectual faculties. The system
of making a student produce a quantity of work
under the pretext of "getting his hand in" is a
very indifferent one for most pupils, since it accus-
toms them to write any kind of stuff and to be
satisfied with everything that flows from their pens,
provided the result is copious. Working in this
way, they form no notion of the elemental part
played by that faculty of the intelligence called *taste*,
the mission of which is to determine the choice of
materials as well as their symmetrical arrangement;
and it is to this error that we must attribute the
production of the numerous works—as compendious
in thought as they are useless to art—which invade
the stage and the concert-room, not only in France,
but in Germany and Italy.

"Do not write much, but let it be very good,"

" Father " Franck used to say, and the strength of his school has been the maintenance of this precept.

When we had finished our study of counterpoint, which he always demanded should be melodic and intelligent, and a course of fugue, in which he advised his students to seek for *expression* rather than mere combination, he was then prepared to initiate us into the mysteries of composition, which, according to him, was entirely based upon tonal construction.

No art, in fact, bears a closer relation to music than that of construction—architecture. In the erection of an edifice it is first of all necessary that the materials should be of good quality and chosen with discernment; in the same way a composer must be very particular in the selection of his musical *ideas* if he wishes to create a lasting work. But in building it is not sufficient to have fine materials without the knowledge how to dispose them so that by their cohesion they shall form a strong and harmonious whole. Stones, no matter how carefully hewn, can never form a monumental edifice if they are simply superimposed upon each other without due order; neither will musical phrases, however beautiful in themselves, constitute a great work unless their distribution and concatenation follow some definite and logical order. Only on these conditions can the structure be raised, and if the elements are good and the synthetic order harmoniously contrived the work will be solid and enduring.

Musical composition is just the same. This is what Franck—and perhaps no one else at that time—knew how to make his pupils realise. In practice he adhered essentially to the laws of form, while leaving us complete liberty in the application of them. Thanks to his habit, to which I have already referred, of seeking in each student the special quality to be cultivated for the profit of his art, his instruction was exceedingly liberal-minded ; for, while he respected as much as any one the highest laws of our art—the laws of nature and of tradition —he applied them intelligently, reconciling them with those rights of individual initiative which he always left his pupils free to exercise. Severe as he was in pointing out the faults of form and the scamped workmanship which undermine the very foundations of a work of art, he was equally indulgent to faults in detail or failure to observe the letter of the law as laid down by the Schools. When this failure seemed to him justifiable, he would say with a smile that was more genial than ironical : " They would not permit you to do that at the Conservatoire—but I like it very much."

At the same time his courage in admitting everything that seemed to him *good* did not blind him to defects of style. If, after searching investigation, he could not conscientiously approve a disputed passage, he was careful only to say to the student, "That is not good ; you must bring it to me again," like any other professor ; only Franck went into the reasons for its not being good, and explained them so clearly that the pupil could not fail to be convinced.

One of the most valuable features of Franck's lessons was his demonstration by example. If we were perplexed in the arrangement of our work, involved in some difficulty in the progress of a composition, the master would at once fetch from his library some score by Bach, Beethoven, Schumann, or Wagner. "Look," he would say, "Beethoven (or some other composer) finds himself here just in the same situation as yours. Now see how he gets out of it. Read these passages, and find inspiration to correct your work ; but do not imitate—try to find your own solution of the difficulty."

May I be allowed to relate an anecdote bearing upon this ? It is of course personal, because it refers to the way in which I became " Father " Franck's pupil, but it gives an idea of his engaging frankness.

After I had played him a movement of my quartet (which I fondly imagined to be of such a nature as to win his approbation), he was silent for a moment ; then, turning to me with a melancholy air, he spoke

the words which I have never been able to forget,
since they had a decisive action upon my life:
" There are some good things in it ; it shows spirit
and a certain instinct for dialogue between the parts ;
the ideas would not be bad—but—that is not enough ;
the work is not finished—in fact, *you really know
nothing whatever.*" Seeing that I was dreadfully
mortified by this opinion, for which I was not at all
prepared, he went on to explain his reasons, and
wound up by saying : " Come to see me, if you
want us to work together. I could teach you composition."

When I got home—the interview took place very
late in the evening—I lay awake at night, rebelling
against the severity of this sentence, but agitated in
the depths of my heart, and I said to myself that
Franck was an old-fashioned musician who knew
nothing of a young and progressive art. Nevertheless, the next day, having calmed down, I took up
my unfortunate quartet and went over, one by one,
the observations which the master had made, emphasising his words the while, according to his custom,
by innumerable arabesques scrawled in pencil over
the manuscript, and I was obliged to own to myself
that he was perfectly right—I knew nothing. I
went to him, almost in fear and trembling, to ask
if he would be good enough to take me as a pupil,
and he admitted me to the organ class at the

Conservatoire, of which he had just been appointed professor.

This class, which I always remember with emotion, was for a long time the true centre for the study of composition at the Conservatoire. At that period (I am speaking of the far-away years from 1872 onward) the three courses of *advanced composition* were taken by the following masters : Victor Massé, composer of comic operas, who had no notion of symphonic music, and who, being constantly ill, was in the habit of passing on his duties to one of his pupils ; Henri Reber, an elderly musician of narrow and old-fashioned views ; finally, François Bazin, who had no idea of what musical composition meant. It is not astonishing, therefore, that César Franck's lofty teaching, based upon Bach and Beethoven, but admitting all new and generous impulses and aspirations, should have attracted all the young spirits endowed with noble ideas and really enamoured of their art. In this way the master almost unconsciously drew off all the truly artistic forces scattered through the various classes in the Conservatoire, not to mention the pupils outside who went for their lessons to his quiet room in the Boulevard Saint-Michael, the high windows of which gave out upon a shady garden—a rare occurrence in Paris. Here we gathered once a week ; for " Father " Franck was not contented with instructing us at his organ class, in fugue, counterpoint, and improvisation ; he invited to his house such of his pupils as seemed worthy of some special teaching, and this was done in an entirely disinterested spirit, which is not usual among professors of public institutions, in which the gratuitous instruction announced in the prospectus is, alas ! far from being a reality.

Such was Franck's affection for his disciples that he never neglected any opportunity of proving it, or even of giving them any information which he thought would interest them. When, after the fatigues of the day, he had said good-bye to those he was in the habit of receiving in the evening, he frequently sat down at his writing-table, not to compose or orchestrate, but to write—often at great length— to his pupils in the provinces, drawing up, with the greatest care, instructions and advice for their benefit.

I cannot refrain from quoting one example of this affectionate solicitude, although it concerns me personally.

Having been summoned to Antwerp, on the occasion of the exhibition of 1885, in order to conduct some of his works at a festival concert, the programme of which included a little composition by his pupil, he still found time, amid all his occupations, to write me this letter, wherein he speaks far more of others than of himself :

"ANTWERP, *Friday, August* 14.

" MY DEAR VINCENT,

" A thousand thanks for your kind and affectionate letter. I need hardly say that it is one of those that gave me the greatest pleasure.*

" I will write you a longer letter another time, but I want to tell you that at a concert here your 'Chevauchée du Cid' was played *perfectly*, and had a great success. Fontaine sang the solo. You were in the same company as your master, whose march and ballet music from ' Hulda ' were warmly applauded.

" I must say good-bye, my dear Vincent. Give my kindest remembrances to your dear wife.

" A kiss to the charming children.

" Duparc is *established* near Pau. He has *bought* a property.

                    "Your old friend,
                        "CÉSAR FRANCK."

In spite of his natural affability, Franck was regarded with suspicion by most of the musicians of his day, and as, notwithstanding his modesty, he could never bring himself to cringe to the powers that be, any more than he would conform in a flabby way to the sacrosanct regulations of the Conservatoire when it seemed to him necessary that they should be broken, he was, throughout his career, the object of

---

* He had just been made Chevalier of the Legion of Honour.

the envy and hatred of his colleagues, who evidently misunderstood him, because his mind was in every way the exact opposite of theirs.

This hatred sometimes extended to his pupils—a more serious matter, since I have known competitions in which prizes were withheld from those who most deserved them, merely in order to spite the professor. The next day our good " Father " Franck, who never suspected an injustice, would be so far from blaming the jury that he innocently helped us to seek out all the faults that might have brought about this adverse decision.

It is not within the limits of my subject to find fault with the lack of culture among the students of the Conservatoire at this time, a deficiency which, it must be confessed, was due to their teachers. It will be sufficient to say that while they were completely ignorant of all the music of the sixteenth and seventeenth centuries, and of a great part of the work of the eighteenth, they usually regarded Bach as a bore, and Gluck's style was the butt of their wittiest jokes. They found consecutive fifths in " Armide," and—*proh pudor!*— declared they had discovered them also in a fugue sent up for competition by Franck himself! At the present moment a change has come over the spirit of the Conservatoire, and every student of composition would consider himself dishonoured

unless he embellished his efforts with a multitude
of more or less conspicuous consecutive fifths.
At the time of which I am speaking Bizet's
" Carmen," which had just been performed, found
no grace in the sight of these critics, and I knew
students of composition who then accused this work
of excessive Wagnerism, while others turned away
their eyes from so coarse a subject and cried " Fie ! "
at the top of their voices. Finally there were some
who deliberately refused to read any music, even
the greatest masterpieces, for fear, so they said, of
" weakening their individuality " !

Of all this Franck knew nothing, and in spite
of the conventional errors of the schools, he continued to exhort his pupils to read a great deal
of fine music, old and new. He himself was as
enthusiastic as any youth over the absolute beauty
of Bach's works, which he taught us to interpret
on the organ.

Neither could he have understood—and would
have been very much surprised to hear it proclaimed
as a discovery—that Art ought to be the expression of Life—as though Art ever had been or could
be anything else ! As though the frescoes of Giotto
or Gozzoli, Rembrandt's Syndics, the west door of
Amiens Cathedral, Beethoven's sonatas, and Gluck's
music dramas were not just as admirable "slices
of life " as the most modern works of art—I

mean, of course, those that spring from the artist's
heart.   But, according to the naïve partisans of this
aphorism,* the word " life" dispenses us from all
preliminary study ; we can all be born architects
and raise up a monumental edifice without having
learnt to balance the weight of our material;
every one of us guided by "inspiration" could
write a symphony straight away.   These are things
that the mind of Franck was incapable of grasp-
ing ; his art, the outcome of long study and creative suffering, is the antithesis of the theories
described above.

At the same time, how truly vital, throbbing
with a sane and intense vitality, is the work of
César Franck !   How ardently he expresses the
joys and griefs which he sees around him.   Not
merely does he interpret in music the life and emotions of others, but he expresses himself.   What
does it matter that the characters in *The Beatitudes* are not represented in modern dress, if we,
men and women of to-day, are profoundly touched
by the sublime invocation to eternal justice ; if we
ourselves suffer with the persecuted, and if we discern the soul of our beloved master in the melodies
he devoted with such tenderness to the description
of meekness and purity ?

Undoubtedly Franck's art was all compounded of
* "Tranches de Vie."

goodness and absolute sincerity, just as his teaching was all love and charity, and on this account it will live ; for Doubt and Hatred, although they may have sometimes destroyed useful things, have never constructed anything endurable. Love and Faith can alone conceive and bring forth an immortal work.

II

THE ARTISTIC FAMILY

THE influence of so excellent a master as César
Franck could not fail to make itself felt among the
future composers who spent some time in his organ
class, such as Samuel Rousseau, who was his assistant
choir-master for many years at Sainte-Clotilde;
Gabriel Pierné, who was nominated organist of the
basilica on his master's death; Auguste Chapuis,
whose efforts have helped to popularise good music
among the masses; H. Dallier and A. Dutacq;
Georges Marty, the young and daring conductor of
the old Société des Concerts; Galeotti, A. Mahaut,
G. Saint-Réné-Taillandier, Ch. Tournemire, and Paul
Vidal, the clever conductor of the Grand Opéra.

The spirit of Franck also reacted on some of his
colleagues on the Committee of the Société Nationale
de Musique : his friend Al. Guilmant, Emmanuel
Chabrier, who was deeply attached to him, Paul
Dukas, and Gabriel Fauré himself, without counting
other executive artists, such as Paul Braud, Armand
Parent, and the great violinist Ysaye.

But it was more especially that circle of private pupils to whom he gave lessons in his own home in the Boulevard Saint-Michel who helped to establish and maintain the lofty traditions of his teaching and to prove its excellence in their own works.

The title *a pupil of Franck*, which we now claim as an honour, was not always regarded as such—far from it. I knew the time when a young composer who had ventured to the Boulevard Saint-Michel to ask some advice from the master, *just to see what it was like,* would have looked down his nose had he been questioned as to his relations with the organist of Sainte-Clotilde, and would willingly have replied, like St. Peter before the High Priest: " I know not the man."

And now that the master has joined the Immortals, his pupils have suddenly become legion, and the majority of the composers of his day pretend that they drank at the source of his wise and fruitful teaching. There are scarcely any opera- or balladmongers of the last ten years who do not advertise themselves at his expense ; although the style of their productions leaves no room for doubt on this point.

It seems to me, therefore, that it would be a useful thing to compile in this book a list of the pupils who actually studied composition under Franck. Having known them all and seen them at work, I have no difficulty in drawing up this register, which I will arrange, as far as possible, in chronological order.

The first to work with the master before the war of 1870 were Arthur Coquard, Albert Cahen, and Henri Duparc, the latter an emulator of Schubert and Schumann in the sphere of the *Lied*. Then came Alexis de Castillon, a cavalry officer, who had always been passionately fond of music. He first asked Victor Massé to undertake his musical education; but the composer of "Les Noces de Jeannette" very soon disgusted his pupil by his ridiculously narrow-minded precepts, and the latter was about to abandon music in his discouragement when he met Franck, who instantly discerned the capacities of this exceptional nature. This meeting was a revelation to Castillon, who destroyed all his previous compositions and wrote Op. 1 over his quintet, as the first result of his new studies. We all know what a fine career lay before this gifted composer, a career which was unhappily cut short by his premature death before he had reached his thirty-fifth year.

From 1872 the school of César Franck included: the author of this volume, Camille Benoît, Augusta Holmès, and Ernest Chausson, who was suddenly snatched from his affectionate friends by a terrible accident, leaving behind him work of the highest value, which seemed, however, to promise even greater artistic worth during the last years of his life; then there were Paul de Wailly, Henri Kunkelmann, and Pierre de Brével, that subtle and distinguished craftsman who inherited his master's feeling for architecture; Louis de Serres, in whom Franck particularly admired a delicate gift of expression; Guy Ropartz, a born symphonist, who has remained inseparably attached to Franck's principles, in spite of his official position as Director of the Conservatoire at Nancy; Gaston Vallin; Charles Bordes, head of the Chanteurs de Saint-Gervais and the courageous promoter of the movement to reconstitute church music; finally, poor Guillaume Lekeu, by temperament almost a genius, who died at four-and-twenty, before he could show his gifts in any complete form.

These, and these only, knew the master intimately and were able to assimilate his innermost thoughts and his invigorating counsels; they alone know what César Franck's lessons in composition actually were : a community of effort on the part of master and pupils directed to one identical aim—Art. They alone could bear witness to that almost supernatural communion of spirit which passed like an electric current between themselves and the composer of *The Beatitudes*; for, as one of his biographers has justly observed : " There never was a less exacting professor or one who was listened to with greater attention."* And they will never forget as long as life lasts the spiritual influence of their lamented master.

What more can I say ?

In the three sections of this book I have tried to show the man as I knew him, and to make others love him as I loved him myself ; to win admiration for the creative artist by analysing some of his noblest works ; and, finally, to reveal the great master of composition who transmitted his strength and his faith to a pleiad of French symphonists.

His beneficent influence reaches beyond the grave, for, cherishing the remembrance of his counsels, some of his pupils and friends have founded a school in which they pride themselves upon teaching younger spirits to walk with uplifted heads, keeping a straight course in the one wholesome way of Art, just as their old master taught them in their turn.†
Speaking of this radiant influence which still shines upon and strengthens many who only started life after the composer of *The Beatitudes* had passed away, a musician who was not among his pupils, but who is equally sincere as a critic as he is as a composer, says : "I have already called attention

* G. Derepas, " César Franck."
† The *Schola Cantorum*, founded in 1896 by Al. Guilmant, Charles Bordes, and Vincent d'Indy.

to the importance of Franck's influence upon the new departure which, since his time, has taken place in contemporary French music. Together with those of Saint-Saëns and Edouard Lalo, his name denotes an epoch. So far, every purely musical development which has come after him has its origin in him, and, thanks to the traditions established by his art, at a moment when Wagnerian influences were on the increase, most of our younger composers have been able to shake off the servile and humiliating yoke imposed by this tendency. They cannot be too grateful to their elders for this, and can find no better means of showing their gratitude than by continuing to spread the great traditions which the School of Franck preserved when it taught that these traditions were above humanity, and far above individual success. " *

I can find no more fitting conclusion for my work than this tribute of respect paid officially and in public to the genius who was also a firm believer :

" Now he is in his own place, among the choir of immortal geniuses who will be our hostages through the future ages, and who constitute, perhaps, the reason of our existence and the justification of humanity in this world." †

* Paul Dukas, *La Chronique des Arts*, 1904, No. 33.

† Extract from the speech made by M. Henry Marcel, Director of the Beaux-Arts, at the unveiling of the monument to César Franck, October 22, 1904.

LIST OF THE WORKS OF
CÉSAR FRANCK

THIS list, which is as complete as possible, has been compiled after long and careful research in various libraries and publishing houses. With the exception of some old manuscripts in the possession of M. Georges C. Franck, I think few omissions will be discovered. I have adopted chronological order in making this catalogue, and it should be understood that I have only included works in their *original form*.

[In the body of the book I have used English titles, but have adhered to the French in the List of Works as being more convenient for purposes of reference.—TRANSLATOR.]

Opus No.	Date of Composition	Titles of Works	Dedications	Original Edition	Present Edition (1906)	Remarks
		First Epoch				
1	1841	*Trois trios concertans* for piano, violin, and violoncello 1st trio in F#. 2nd trio in B♭ (trio de salon). 3rd trio in B	To H. M. M. Leopold I., King of the Belgians	Schuberth and Co.	Schuberth, Leipzig	—
2	1842	*Quatrième trio concertant* for piano, violin, and violoncello	To his friend Franz Liszt	Schuberth	Schuberth	—
3	1842	*Eglogue* (Hirtengedicht)	To Mme. la Baronne de Chabannes	Schlésinger	—	Edition exhausted
4	1842	*Duo* for four hands on " God save the King " for piano	To Mlles. Anna and Emmeline Stratton	Schlésinger	—	Edition exhausted
5	1843	*Grand caprice* for piano	To Mme. Cordier	Lemoine	Lemoine	—
6	1843	*Andante quietoso*, for piano and violin	To M. le Comte de Montendre	Lemoine	Lemoine	—
7	1843	*Souvenir d' Aix-la-Chapelle*, for piano	To Mlle. Cécile Lachambre	Schuberth	—	Edition exhausted

			To Mlle. Cécile Lachambre	E. Challiot		
8	1844	Quatre mélodies de Schubert, transcribed for piano / 1. La jeune religieuse / 2. La truite / 3. Les plaintes de la jeune fille / 4. La cloche des agonisants	To Mlle. Cécile Lachambre	—	—	The MSS. only preserved
9	1844	Ballade, for piano	—	?	—	No trace of this work to be found anywhere
10	1844	Solo de piano, with string quartet accompaniment	—	?	—	
11	1844	Première fantaisie sur Gulistan, de Dalayrac, for piano	—	Richault	Costallat	
12	1844	Deuxième fantaisie sur l'air et le Virelay "Le point du jour" de Gulistan, de Dalayrac, for piano	To Mlle. Marguerite Henriette Adour	Richault	Costallat	
13	1844	Fantaisie, for piano	—	?	—	It is supposed that this fantasia was never written; no trace of it exists
14	1844	Duo pour piano et violon concertans on airs from Dalayrac's Gulistan	To Mlle. Félicité de Cécil de Herck Saint-Lambert	Richault	Costallat	
15	1845	Fantaisie pour piano on two Polish airs	To S. A. Mme. la Princesse de Ligne, née Lubomirska	Richault	Costallat	

Opus No.	Date of Composition	Titles of Works	Dedications	Original Edition	Present Edition (1906)	Remarks
16	1845	Trois petits riens, for piano 1. Duellino 2. Valse 3. Le Songe	To S. A, Mme. la Princesse de Ligne, née Lubomirska	?	—	—
17	1846	Duo à quatre mains, for piano, on Grétry's "Lucile"	—	Pacini-Bonaldi	—	Edition exhausted
	towards 1846	Le Sermon sur la montagne, symphony (The Beatitudes)	—	—	—	Un-published
	1843–1846	Ruth, Biblical eclogue in three parts for soli, chorus, and orchestra	—	Hartmann (1872)	Heugel	—
		Souvenance (Chateaubriand), melody	To Mme. Pauline Viardot	Richault	Costallat	—
	1842–1843	Ninon (A. de Musset), melody	To Dr. Féréol	Richault	Costallat	—
		L'émir de Bengador (Méry), melody	To Mme. Louise Boutet de Monvel	Richault	Costallat	On cover, "To M. Alphonse Boutet de Monvel"
		Le Sylphe (Al. Dumas), melody with 'cello obbligato	To Mme. Claire Brissaud	Richault	Costallat	—
		Robin Gray (Florian), melody	To Mme. Claire Brissaud	Richault	Costallat	—

		To Mme. César Franck	?	Hamelle (1878)	
1846	*L'ange et l'enfant* (Reboul), melody	—	?	—	—
1851–1852	*Le valet de ferme*, comic opera in three acts on poem by Alphonse Royer and Gustave Vaes	—	—	—	Un-published
1852	*Les trois exilés*, national song for baritone and bass	—	Mayaud	—	Edition exhausted
	SECOND EPOCH				
1858	*Messe solennelle* for bass solo and organ. (*O salutaris*, extract from the Mass)	—	Régnier-Canaux	—	Edition exhausted
1858	*Andantino*, for organ	—	Richault	Costallat	—
1858	*Accompagnement d'orgue* and arrangement for voices of the Gregorian services restored by Father Lambillotte. 2nd, 3rd, 4th, and 5th parts	—	Ad. Le-clère	—	—
1858	*O Salutaris*, duet for soprano and tenor	—	Régnier-Canaux	Noël	—
1858	*Trois motets* 1. *O salutaris*, for soprano and chorus 2. *Ave Maria*, duet for soprano and bass 3. *Tantum ergo*, for bass	—	„	Noël	—

Opus No.	Date of Composition	Titles of Works	Dedications	Original Edition	Present Edition (1906)	Remarks
	1859	*Trois antiennes*, for grand organ	—	Hartmann	Heugel	—
	1859	*Le Garde d'honneur*, hymn (nine verses)	—	Régnier-Canaux	Noel	—
12	1860	*Messe à trois voix*, for soprano, tenor, and bass, with organ, harp, cello and double-bass accompaniment	—	Repos	Borne-mann (1872)	—
16	1860–1862	*Six pièces pour grand orgue* 1. Fantaisie in C . .	To his friend M.A.Chauvet	Maeyens-Couvreur	Durand (1879)	—
17		2. Grande Pièce Symphonique .	To M.Ch.Val-entin Alkan			
18		3. Prélude, fugue, et variation .	To his friend M. C. Saint-Saëns			
19		4. Pastorale	To his friend M. Aristide Cavaillé Coll			
20		5. Prière	To his master M. Benoist			
21		6. Final	To his friend M. Lefébure-Wély			

22		To Mlle. Marie-Thérèse Miccio		Leduc	
1862	*Quasi marcia* for harmonium .	To Mlle. Marie-Thérèse Miccio	Graff	Leduc	—
1863	*Cinq pièces* for harmonium Two offertoires Two versets One communion	—	Graff-Parvy	Leduc	—
1863	*Ave Maria*, for soprano, tenor, and bass	—	Repos	Borne-mann	—
1863	*44 petites pièces*, for organ or harmonium	—	—	Enoch (1900)	Published under the title "Posthumous Pieces"
1865	*La tour de Babel*, short oratorio for soli, chorus, and orchestra	—	—	—	Unpublished.
1865	*Les plaintes d'une poupée*, for piano	To Mlle. Gabrielle Œsch-ger	—	Mangeot	MSS. dated April 18, 1865
1870	*Paris*, patriotic song for tenor with orchestra	—	—	—	Unpublished
1871	*Trois offertoires* 1. *Quæ est ista*, for the festival of	—	Repos	Borne-mann	—

Opus No.	Date of Composition	Titles of Works	Dedications	Original Edition	Present Edition	Remarks
		the Virgin; for soli, chorus, organ, and double-bass				
		2. *Domine Deus in simplicitate*; for the first Sunday in the month; for three voices, organ, and double-bass				
		3. *Dextera Domini*, for Easter Sunday; for soli, chorus in three parts, organ, and double-bass	To M. l'abbé Hamelin, curé of Ste.-Clotilde		Enoch	—
	1871	*Le mariage des roses* (E. David), melody	To Mme. Trélat	—	Bornemann	—
	1871	*Domine non secundum*, offertory for Lent ; trio for soprano, tenor, and bass	—	Le Courrier des familles	Bornemann	
	1871	*Quasi fremuerunt gentes*, offertory for the festival of Saint Clotilde ; chorus for three voices, organ, and double-bass	—	Le Bailly		
	1871	*Offertoire*, for harmonium, on a Breton air	—	Nauss	—	—

Date	Work	Dedication			Remarks
1872	Panis angelicus, for tenor, organ, harp, cello and double-bass	—	Le Bailly	Bornemann	Interpolated in the Mass for 3 voices
1871	Rédemption, symphonic poem for soprano solo, chorus, and orchestra (poem by Ed. Blau). Pianoforte score by the composer	—	Hartmann (1872)	Heugel	First version
1872	Passez, passez toujours (V. Hugo), melody	—	—	Costallat	—
1872	Roses et papillons (V. Hugo), melody	To Alexis de Castillon	—	Enoch	—
1872	Veni creator, duet for tenor and bass	To MM.Verg-net and Menu	Echo des maîtrises, 1st book	Hamelle	—
1873	Lied (Lucien Paté), melody .	To Albert Co-hen (d'Anvers)	—	Enoch	—
1873	Prélude, fugue, et variation, for harmonium and piano	—	Maeyens-Couvreur	Durand	Transcription of the organ piece Op. 18
1874	Rédemption (2nd edition); new symphonic piece and chorus for men added	—	Hartmann (1874)	Heugel	Second version

Opus No.	Date of Composition	Titles of Works	Dedications	Original Edition	Present Edition (1906)	Remarks
		THIRD EPOCH				
	1876	Les Eolides, symphonic poem for orchestra (after the poem by Leconte de Lisle). The original arrangement for pianoforte duet by the composer	—	—	Enoch	—
	1878	Trois pièces pour grand orgue . 1. Fantasia in A 2. Cantabile 3. Pièce heroïque	—	—	Durand	—
	1878–1879	Quintet in F minor, for piano, two violins, viola, and 'cello	To Camille Saint-Saëns	—	Hamelle	—
	1879	Le vase brisé (Sully-Prudhomme), melody			Enoch	—
	1869–1879	Les Béatitudes, oratorio for solo voices, chorus, and orchestra, in eight parts and a prologue. (Poem by Mme. Colomb.) The pianoforte score by the composer	To Mme. César Franck	Brandus	Joubert	—
	1881	Rebecca, Biblical scene for soli, chorus,	To the Amateur	Hartmann	Heugel	—

Date	Work	Dedication		Publisher	
	and orchestra. (Poem by Paul Collin.) Pianoforte score by the composer	ChoralSociety and its founder, Antonin Guillot de Sainbris	—	L. Grus	—
1882	Le Chasseur maudit, symphonic poem for orchestra (after Bürger). The original arrangement for pianoforte duet by the composer	—	—		—
1884	Nocturne (L. de Fourcaud), melody	—	Album du Gaulois (1885)	Enoch	—
1884	Les Djinns, symphonic poem for piano and orchestra (after V. Hugo). Arranged for two pianos by the composer	—	—	Enoch	—
1884	Prélude, choral, et fugue, for piano	To Mlle. Marie Poitevin	—	Enoch	—
1882–1885	Hulda, opera in four acts and an epilogue on a Scandinavian subject. (Poème by Ch. Grandmougin, after Bjornstierne-Björnson)	—	—	Choudens	—

Opus No.	Date of Composition	Titles of Works	Dedication	Original Edition	Present Edition (1906)	Remarks
	1885	*Variations symphoniques,* for piano and orchestra. Arranged by the composer for two pianos	—	—	Enoch	—
	1885	*Danse lente,* for piano	—	Album du Gaulois	Schola Cantorum	—
	1886	*Sonate* for piano and violin	To Eugène Ysaye	—	Hamelle	—
	1886–1887	*Prélude, aria, et final,* for piano	To Mme. Bordes-Pêne	—	Hamelle	—
	1887–1888	*Psyché,* symphonic poem for orchestra and chorus	To my friend Vincent d'Indy	Bruneau	Borne-mann	—
	1888	*Hymne,* for four male voices (Racine)	To Sylvain Dupuis	—	Hamelle	—
	1888	*Cantique,* with chorus	—	—	—	Un-published
	1888	*La Procession* (Brizeux), melody. Original arrangement for orchestra	To Mme. Char-lotte Danner	Bruneau	Leduc	—

		To Maurice Bagès	Bruneau	Leduc	Posthumous work
1888	Les cloches du soir (Daudet), melody	To Maurice Bagès	—	—	—
1888	Psaume CL, for chorus, orchestra, and organ	—	—	Breitkopf and Härtel	—
1888	Six duos, part-songs for equal voices	—	—	Enoch	
	1. L'ange gardien				
	2. Aux petits enfants (A. Daudet)	To Eugène Pierné			
	3. La vierge à la crèche (A. Daudet)	To Mme. Pauline Roger			
	4. Les danses de Lormont (Mme. Desbordes-Valmore)	To Jules Minard			
	5. Soleil (J. Guy Ropartz)	To Charles Pierné			
	6. La chanson du vannier (A. Theuriet)	To Mme. Saint-Louis de Gonzague			
1886–1888	Symphony in D minor for orchestra	To my friend Henri Duparc	—	Hamelle	—
1888	Le premier sourire de mai, chorus for three female voices (V. Wilder)	—	—	Hamelle	—
1889	Andantino, for grand organ	—	Musée de l'organiste, Book IV., 97	Costallat	—

Opus No.	Date of Composition	Titles of Works	Dedications	Original Edition	Present Edition (1906)	Remarks
	1889	*Preludes et prières de Ch. V. Alkan*, selected and arranged for the organ in three books	—	Richault	Costallat	—
	1889	*Quartet in D major* for two violins, viola, and 'cello	To Léon Reynier	—	Hamelle	—
	1888–1890	*Ghisèle*, lyrical drama in four acts. (Poem by Gilbert Augustin Thierry)	—	—	Choudens	Unfinished
	1889–1890	*L'Organiste*, fifty-nine pieces for the harmonium	—	—	Enoch	—
	1890	*Trois chorals*, for grand organ	—			Durand	The real dedications to A. Guilmant, Th. Dubois, E. Gigout
		1. In E .	To M. Eug. Girout			
		2. In B minor .	To M. Aug. Durand			
		3. In A minor .	To Mlle. Augusta Holmès			

BIBLIOGRAPHY OF WORKS AND DOCUMENTS CONSULTED

N.B.—Among the numerous articles from newspapers and periodicals dealing with César Franck, we only give here a list of those which present some æsthetic or historic interest, purposely omitting mere reports of works or concerts.

F. BALDENSPERGER. *César Franck. L'Artiste et sor œuvre.* Edition du Courrier musical (published separately or in the number for May 15, 1901).

CAMILLE BENOÎT. *César Franck.* La Revue Bleue, December 1890.

—— *César Franck.* Revue et Gazette musical, *passim.*

CHARLES BORDES. *Le sentiment religieux dans la musique d'église de Franck.* Courrier musical, November 1, 1904.

RICCIOTTO CANUDO. *C. Franck e la giovane Scuola musicale francese.* Nuova Antologia (published separately). Rome, 1905.

ERNEST CHAUSSON. *César Franck.* Le Passant, 1891.

ARTHUR COQUARD. *César Franck, 1822–1890.* Published 1890 ; 1st edition exhausted. New edition published in Le Monde musical, 1904.

COURRIER MUSICAL. Number of November 1, 1904 (entirely devoted to Franck).

272   BIBLIOGRAPHY

VICTOR DEBAY. *César Franck.* Courrier musical, November 15 and December 1, 1900.

GUSTAVE DEREPAS. *César Franck, Etude sur sa vie, son enseignement, son œuvre.* Fischbacher, 1897.

ETIENNE DESTRANGES. *L'œuvre lyrique de César Franck.* Fischbacher, 1896.

PAUL DUKAS. *Les Béatitudes.* Revue hebdomadaire, vol. xi. p. 302. 1893.

—— *A propos of César Franck.* La Chronique des Arts, No. 33, p. 273. 1904.

A. ELSON. Modern Composers of Europe (p. 132). Page & Co., Boston, 1905.

EMILE GOUDEAU. *César Franck.* Journal la France, November 14, 1890.

LOUIS FR. GUILBERT. *César Franck.* L'Enseignement chrétien (published separately). Poussielgue, 1905.

HUGUES IMBERT. *Portraits et études.* Fischbacher.

VINCENT D'INDY. *César Franck, le premier des symphonistes français.* The Weekly Critical Review, March 5, 1903.

—— *L'œuvre de piano de César Franck.* The Musician. O. Ditson & Co., Boston.

PAUL LOCARD. *Les maîtres modernes de l'orgue.* Edition du Courrier musical.

D. G. MASON. *From Grieg to Brahms* (pp. 124–147). Outlook & Co. New York, 1904.

G. MAUCLAIR. *Impressions sur Franck.* Courrier musical, November 1, 1904.

PHILIPPE MOREAU. *L'âme de Franck.* Monde musical, October 30, 1904.

RENÉ DE RÉCY. *César Franck.* La Revue Bleue, *passim.*

HUGO RIEMANN. *Dictionnaire de Musique,* traduction de G. Humbert, Perrin et Cie.

J. GUY ROPARTZ. *Notations artistiques.* Symphonies modernes (pp. 163–190). Lemerre.

—— *César Franck.* Revue internationale de Musique, June 13, 1898.

—— *Analyse du Quatuor en ré.* Revue internationale de Musique, August 1, 1898.

G. SERVIÈRES. *La musique française moderne.* G. Havard, 1897.

—— *César Franck.* L'Art, March 1, 1891.

W. STUMPF. *Les Béatitudes van C. A. Franck.* Van Munster en Zoon. Amsterdam, 1895.

A. SEITZ. *Le génie de César Franck.* Monde musical, October 30, 1904.

SOUVENIR DU 22 OCTOBRE, 1904. Account of the unveiling of the monument to César Franck, the work of the sculptor Alfred Lenoir, in the garden-square of Sainte-Clotilde ; containing also the text of the speeches and the names of all the subscribers.

A. VAN DEN BORREN. *L'œuvre dramatique de C. Franck,* Bruxelles, 1906.

INDEX

Æneid, Virgil's, 203
Agnus Dei, 140
Air de Ballet, 53
Alkan, C. A., *Préludes et Chants*
Amiens Cathedral, 248
Amsterdam, 210
Ange et l'Enfant, L', 78, 112
Antony and Cleopatra, 14
Antwerp, 265
Appony, Count, 182
Association Artistique, 210
Attendez-moi sous l'orme, 14
Auguez, M., 52, 53
Avignon, 20

BACH, John Sebastian, 21, 69,
    85, 100, 130, 132, 133
    comparison between Franck
        and, 44, 137
    his influence on Franck,
        93, 94, 95, 100, 134, 164,
        242, 244, 248
    his treatment of Christ,
        212
    invents a Chorale Varia-
        tion, 199
    Passions of, 198, 227
    organ work of, 133, 135
        note, 146
    revival of, 10, 11, 18
    works for pianoforte, 162
Bach Society, the French, 20

Balbreck, M., 55 note
Ballade, Op. 9, 35, 93
    analysis of, 118–120
Balleroy, Mme., 53
Balzac, Honoré, 9
Bartolo di Fredi, 76, 176
Bayreuth, 10
Bazin, François, 244
Beatitudes, The, 133, 138, 146,
    160, 171, 249, 255
    First Beatitude, 216
    Second Beatitude, 216
    Third Beatitude, 53, 95,
        217
    Fourth Beatitude, 95, 218
    Fifth Beatitude, 219
    Sixth Beatitude, 221
    Seventh Beatitude, 223
    Eighth Beatitude, 53, 225–
        228
    analysis of, 76–78, 211,
        214–228
    Christ in, 212–214
    composition of, 45, 46, 143,
        169, 209, 210
    culmination of his art, 203,
        228
    cut into sections, 50
    epic nature of, 205, 228
    genesis of, 206
    given by Colonne, 50, 210
    groundwork of, 42

Beatitudes, The—continued
  heard in England, 12
  individuality of, 94
  influence of Beethoven in,
    88
  private performance of,
    49, 50
  text of, 207–209
  use of the fugue in, 216,
    224
Beethoven, Ludwig von, 11, 21,
    54, 69, 83, 162
  Variation-form, 198, 199
  his influence on Franck,
    93, 95, 100, 105, 108,
    109, 133, 134, 137, 140,
    164, 169, 224, 242, 244
  his *Missa Solemnis*, 29, 205
  his *Ninth Symphony*, 206
  his renovation of the sonata
    form, 84–88
  his Sonatas, 185, 248
  influence of Mozart on,
    93
  Quartets of, 43 note, 87,
    95, 108, 133, 182, 184,
    189, 193, 195, 225
  sketch-books of, 98, 100,
    101, 196
Benedictines, musical researches
  of, 130
Benoist, professor of organ in
  Paris, 33, 34, 47
Benoît, Camille, 152, 253
Berlioz, Hector, *Damnation of
  Faust*, 205
  his influence on Vincent
    d'Indy, 15
  his share in the musical
    renaissance, 11
  his treatment of Christ,
    213
  on Beethoven, 86

Berlioz, Hector—*continued*
  popular neglect of, 8
  Traité d'Orchestration, 135
Beyle, G., 53
Bizet, Georges, 9
  Carmen, 248
Blau, Edouard, 47, 142
Boecklin, Arnold, 80
Bonn, 29, 44
Bordeaux, 20
Bordes, Charles, 17, 254, 255
  note
  on Franck's church music,
    130–132
Bordes-Pène, Mme., 168
Boston, U.S.A., 114 note
Botticelli, Sandro, 122
Brahms, Johannes, influence of,
    16
  debt to Beethoven, 87
  his reception of the *Re-
    demption*, 112
  quartets of, 184
Brand, Paul, 56, 251
Bret, Gustave, 20
Brével, Pierre de, 110 note,
    254
Bridoison, 73
Bruneau, M., on Franck and
  the musical renaissance, 10,
  11
Brussels, 15, 110

Cahen, Albert, 253
Cantabile in B major, 161
Cantata, form of the, 202
Canudo, Ricciotto, on Franck's
  religious music, 142
Cardiff, 12
Castillon, Alexis de, 46, 194, 253
Caters, Mme. de, 153
Cavaillé-Coll, Aristide, 41, 135,
  161

César Franck, by A. Coquard, 93 note
César Franck, étude sur sa vie, son enseignement, son œuvre, 81, 82, 238, 255 note
Chabannes, Baroness, 117
Chabrier, Emmanuel, 251
on the *Redemption*, 157
oration on Franck, 59, 228
Chamber music, 184, 189
Chant de la Cloche, Le, 15
Chanteurs de Saint-Gervais, 17, 18, 254
Chapuis, Auguste, 251
Chasseur Maudit, Le, 52, 161
Chausson, Ernest, 180 note, 195 note, 253
Cherubini, Salvador, 95
examines Franck, 32–34
Chopin, F. F., 89, 113
Chorale, definition of a, 198—
see Organ Chorale
Chronique des Arts, La, 256 note
Collège de Vaugiraud, 94
Colomb, Mme., 208
Colonne Concerts, 173
Colonne, Edouard, 47, 151
his orchestra, 14
produces *The Beatitudes,* 50, 210
Composition, three stages of, 97–99
Concerts Lamoureux, 15
Populaires, 14
Spirituels, 47, 151
Coquard, Arthur, 46, 180 note, 253
reminiscences of Franck, 67, 93
Cornelius, Peter, 78
Cossmann, Herr, 111 note
Courrier Musical, Le, 130 note

Cyclic style, Franck's creation of, 91, 171

DALAYRAC, 92
Dallier, H., 59 note, 251
Damnation de Faust, La, 87, 205
David, Félicien, *Le Désert,* 37
Death of Wallenstein, 14
Degas, M., 65
Delaborde, M., 112
Delibes, Léo, 59 note, 67
Denis, M., 208
Derepas, Gustave, *César Franck,* 238, 285
on Franck's religion, 81
on *Psyche,* 174–176
Désert, Le, 37
Desmousseaux, Madame, 38
Dialogus per la Pascua, 212 note
Diémer, Louis, 13, 52, 169 note
Dies Iræ, 172
Divine Comedy, The, 203, 206
Djinns, Les, 12, 163
Domine non secundum, 130
Dorel, Abbé, 41
Dubois, Théodore, 138, 198 note
Dugas, M., 53
Dukas, Paul, 251
on Franck's Classicism, 83
on Franck's individuality, 89
on Franck's influence, 256
Dumas, Alexandre, 9
Duo à quatre mains, Op. 17, 126
Duo on " God Save the King," 126
Duparc, Henri, 46, 94, 152, 154, 179, 246, 253
Dutacq, A., 251

Eclogue, Op. 3 (Hirtengedicht), 35, 117, 118
Elgar, Edward, 11, 22
Eolides, Les, 48, 161
    Wagnerian influence in, 96
Epic form, the, 202
Epinal, 20
Etranger, L', 15
Euphrosine and Coradin, 93
Euryanthe, 94
Eve, Massenet's, 79

Fantasia for Pianoforte, Op. 13, 125
Fantasia in C, 133
Fantasias upon Gulistan, 125, 126
Fauré, Gabriel, 251
Faust, Gounod's, 54
Ferréot, Dr., 59 note
Fervaal, 15
Figaro, The, 46
Finale in B flat major, 137
Fioretti of St. Francis, 174
Flying Dutchman, The, 104
Fontaine, M., 246
Forêt Enchantée, La, 14
Fornarina, La, 76
Fra Angelico, 222
France, music in, under the Second Empire, 8, 11
    revival of music in, since 1870, 9
Franck, César
    The Man and the Teacher—
    birth of, 29
    artistic inheritance, 30
    destined for the musical profession, 31
    meets Pauline Garcia in Belgium, 31
    enters the Paris Conservatoire, 31

Franck, César—*continued*
    transposes Hummel's Concerto, 32
    wins prizes for fugue, 32, 33
    competes for the organ prize, 33
    leaves the Conservatoire, 34, 110
    meets Liszt, 110
    as a virtuoso, 35, 120
    returns to Paris, 1844, 36
    his eclogue *Ruth* performed, 37
    marriage of, 38
    poverty of, 39
    overworks in writing *Le Valet de Ferme*, 40
    appointed organist of S.-Jean-S. François au Marais, 41
    appointed organist of Sainte-Clotilde, 41, 42
    as an improvisator, 43, 44
    engaged in composition of *The Beatitudes*, 45, 48, 169, 209
    writes the Ode to Paris, 46
    appointed Professor of Organ at the Conservatoire, 47, 244
    writes the *Redemption*, 47, 209
    arranges a private performance of *The Beatitudes*, 49
    divides the work into sections, 50
    receives Governmental distinctions, 51, 52, 246 note
    the festival in his honour, 52, 53

Franck, César—*continued*
his *Symphony* performed,
54, 55
his *String Quartet* per-
formed, 55, 56
elected president of the
Société Nationale de
Musique, 55
his triumph at Tournai,
56
his accident, 56
unable to preside at the
second performance of
the *String Quartet*, 57
death of, 58
funeral of, 58
monument to, 60, 256
note
tardy recognition of, 60,
61
personal appearance of,
62, 63
portrait of, 63 note
his capacity for work, 63–
66, 97
his interest in literature,
64
modesty of, 65
kindly nature of, 66–68,
238, 247
his simple faith, 68, 69,
250
his wrath at bad music,
67, 241
as a teacher, 234–249, 254,
255
his title of " Father," 235
his pupils, 251–255
The Artist and his Music—
musical renaissance due to,
10, 11, 20
influence in France, 10, 20,
235, 256

Franck, César—*continued*
influence in England, 11,
12, 21
influence in Belgium, 12,
21
revives classical forms, 12
his views of *form*, 71, 241
his affinity with fourteenth
and fifteenth century
painters, 76, 176, 212,
222
his artistic conscience, 77
spiritual conceptions of,
78, 173–176, 212, 250
architectural balance of his
work, 80, 90, 171, 241
his mysticism compared
with the Wagnerian,
81
contemplative tendency of,
82
classicism of, 83–85
individuality of, 88, 89, 94
analysis of his style, 90
early predilections of, 92
influence of Bach on, 93–
95, 134
influence of Beethoven on,
87, 88, 93, 95, 105, 108,
109, 133, 134, 137, 140,
164, 169, 224
influence of Gluck on, 94
influence of Liszt on, 105
influence of Méhul on,
93, 105, 120
influence of Meyerbeer on,
96, 121, 215
influence of Schubert on,
94, 110
influence of Wagner on,
96, 134
influence of Weber on, 94,
110

Franck, César—*continued*
  his methods of work, 100–102
  three distinct styles of, 102
  his first period of composition, 104–124
  his *Trios*, 104–112
  his *L'ange et L'Enfant*, 112, 113
  his first pianoforte pieces, 113–120
  his *Ruth* analysed, 120–124
  his second period of composition, 125–158
  his system of cataloguing, 125–127
  religious character of his work, 127–133
  his organ works, 132–142
  his *Redemption* considered, 142–158
  third period of composition, 159–181
  his self-confidence, 160
  his *Cantabile in B ;* the *Quintet in F minor*, 161
  his return to composition for the pianoforte, 161–169
  his *Sonata in A for Violin and Piano*, 169
  establishes the cyclical form, 171
  devotes himself to symphonic form, 171–173
  his *Psyche* and its spirituality, 173–176
  his delight in the *Magnificat*, 176–178
  his attempts at dramatic music, 178–180
  his *Quartet* in D major, 184–197

Franck, César—*continued*
  his organ *Chorales*, 198–201
  culmination of his art in *The Beatitudes*, 206, 228
  composition of, 208–210
  analysis of, 211–228
  list of works of, 257–270
  bibliography of, 271–273
" Franck Festival," The, 52
Franck, Jerome, 30 note
  Joseph, 36
  M. Georges César, 30, 34 note, 37 note, 41 note, 55 note, 63 note, 119, 207 note, 257
Franco-Prussian War, 9, 14, 45, 46
Frescobaldi, 133
Fugue, decline of the, 85

GADDI, Taddeo, 76
Galeotti, 251
Garcia, Pauline, 31
Garcin, Jules, 54
Gardey, Mgr., 42 note, 58, 177
Gautier, Théophile, 9
Gavioli, Mlle., 52, 53
Germany fails to appreciate Franck, 80
  fails to follow Beethoven's lead, 87
Ghisèle, 65, 178–180
Gibier, M., 55 note
Gigout, E., 198 note
Giotto, 248
Giovanni da Fiesole, 78
Glasgow, 12
Gluck, Christopher Willibald, 11, 18, 248
  Armide, 247
  influence on Franck, 94
God save the King, Duet on, 126

Gœthe's *Faust*, 205
Goncourt, Edmond et Jules de, 9
Gounod, Charles, 67
   Faust, 54
   on the *Symphony*, 55
   quartets of, 86
Gozzoli, 248
Grande Pièce Symphonique, 134, 135
Grandval, Mme. de, 153
Gregorian music, 17, 130, 198
Grétry, 92
Grieg, Edvard, on quartets, 183
Grieux, Des, 123
Griset, J., 112
Guilmant, Al., 17, 198 note, 251, 255 note
Guiraud, Ernest, 51
Gulistan, 92 note

Halévy, Fromenthal, *La Juive*, 121
   overtures of, 86
Handel, concertos of, 135 note
   his treatment of Christ, 212
Haydn, F. J., 54, 85, 162
Henri III., 30 note
Hereford, 12
Herrenthal, 30 note
Heymann, M. L., 55 note
Hirten-Gedicht. See *Eclogue*, Op. 3
Holmès, Augusta, 253
Homer, 203, 205
Hugo, Victor, *Les Djinns*, 9, 163
Hulda, 53, 169, 178, 246
   ballet of, 179
Hummel, J. N., A minor concerto, 32
Imbert, M. Hugues, on M. d'Indy, 15

Independent, The, 183 note
Indy, Vincent d', his qualifications as biographer, 7, 11, 13
   at the Queen's Hall Symphony Concert, 1909, 12, 14
   birth of, 13
   studies under Diémer and Lavignac, 13, 14
   shares in the defence of Paris, 14, 46
   becomes a pupil of Franck, 14, 16, 46, 242–244, 253
   choirmaster to Colonne, 14
   produces *The Piccolomini*, 14
   his Trilogy on Wallenstein and other works, 14
   style of, 15–17
   founds the *Schola Cantorum*, 17, 255 note
   ideals of, 18, 19
   as principal of the *Schola*, 18–20
   plays in the first performance of *The Beatitudes*, 49
   takes *Redemption* to Liszt and Brahms in Weimar, 112
   recopies score of *Redemption*, 152
   suggests transposition of *Redemption*, 154
   Psyche dedicated to, 173
   completes *Ghisèle*, 180
   Franck's letter to, 246
   his *Chevauchée du Cid*, 246
Ingres, J. A. D., 90
Iphigénie en Tauride, 94
Italy, musical degeneracy of, 86

JONCIÈRES, Victorin, 50
Joseph, Méhul's, 38, 92, 122
Judaic school of opera, 86

KANT, Emmanuel, *Critic of Pure
    Reason*, 64
Kapellmeister compositions, 129
Kempis, Thomas à, 79
Klopstock's *Messiah*, 204
Kunkelmann, Henri, 254

La Juive, 121
Lalo, Edouard, 50, 153, 256
    Symphony in G minor, 172
Lamartine, Alphonse de, 9
Lamoureux, 48
Laub, Herr, 111 note
Lavignac, 14
Leborne, M., 31
Lefébure-Wély, M., 137
Leipzig Conservatoire, 183
Lekeu, Guillaume, 254
Leopold I., 36, 105
Leslino, Mme., 53
Liège, 29, 31, 106, 210
Liègeois, M. C., 55 note
Lippi, Filippo, 76, 78, 222
Lisle, Leconte de, 48
Liszt, Franz, 35, 88
    his interest in Franck's
        Trios, 110–112
    influence on Franck, 16,
        105, 207
    visits Franck at Ste.
        Clotilde, 44, 137
    writes on three staves, 118
    writes for pianoforte, 162
Lodoïska, 32
Lohengrin, 79
Louis XIV., 128
Loys, M., 161
Lucan's *Pharsalus*, 204
Lyons, 20

Madame Turlupin, 51
Magnificat, 176, 177
Mahaut, A., 251
Malherbe, M. Charles, 114
    note
Manon, 123
Marcel, Henri, on Franck, 256
March, 53
Marie-Magdeleine, Massenet's,
    79
Marseilles, 20
Marsick, M., 161
Marty, Georges, 251
Mason, Dr., 111 note
Mass in D minor, 141
Massé, Victor, 51, 244, 253
Massenet, M., 79 note, 122
Mauclair, Camille, *La Religion
    de la Musique*, 19
    his Views on Franck, 19–
        23
Méhul, influence on Franck,
    105, 120
    Joseph, 38, 92, 122
Meistersinger, 100
Mélodies, Franck's, 126
Memories of a Musical Life, 111
    note
Mendelssohn, Félix Bartholdy,
    83, 87
Messe à trois voix, Op. 12, 126
    analysed, 137–142
Messe solennelle, 130, 141
Messiah, The, 204
Meyerbeer, Giacomo, influence
    on Franck, 96, 121, 215,
    224
    marches of, 86
    popularity of, 8
Minister of Fine Arts, 49, 51
Missa Solemnis, 87, 140, 205
Monde Musical, 93 note
Monsigny, *Le Déserteur*, 92

Monte Carlo, 179, 180
Monteverde, *Orfeo* and *Incoronazione di Poppea*, 20 note
Montluçon, 20
Montpellier, 20
Mozart, W. A., 93, 162
    quartets of, 182
Music, origin of, 127
Musician, The, 15

NANCY, 20, 254
New York, 111 note
Nibelungen, The, 81, 134, 205
Noces de Jeannette, Les, 61, 253
Notations Artistiques, 173 note
Nuova Antologia, 142 note

ONSLOW, quintets of, 86
Oratorio, history of the, 202–206
Orcagna, Andrea, 122
Organ Chorales, Franck's, 54, 58, 88, 160
    in A, 201
    in B, 201
    in E, 198–201
Organiste, L', 59 *Pièces pour Harmonium* 176
Orientales, Les, 163 note

PADUA, Arena of, 174
Palestrina, Pierluigi, 18, 19, 69, 131, 132
Paradise Lost, 204
Parent, Armand, 251
Paris, Boulevard S. Michel, 10
    Cirque des Champs Elysées, 38
    Cirque d'Hiver, 52
    Conservatoire, 14
    concerts of, 210
        Franck professor of organ at, 47, 244
        Franck studies at, 31–34

Paris—*continued*
    neglect of Franck, 47, 49, 59, 61, 247
    tuition at, 233, 236, 247
    Franck's ode on, 46
    N. D. de Lorette, 38, 41
    Revolution of 1848, 38
    Sainte Clotilde, 41–44, 58, 132, 251
    Sainte Jacques, 58
    S.-Jean-S. François au Marais, 41
    Sainte Valère, 41
    siege of, 14, 46
    Théâtre Lyrique, 68
    Trocadéro, 161
Parsifal, 96, 104
Pasdeloup, Jules, 52, 53
    produces *The Piccolomini*, 14
Pastorale, 136
Pau, 246
Perugino, Paolo Vanucci, 76
Pharsalus, 204
Pianoforte, works for, 162
Piccolomini, The, 14
Pierné, Gabriel, 251
Poitevin, Mme., 164
Prélude, Aria, and Finale, 168, 169
    Choral et Fugue, 96 note
    analysis of, 163–168
    Fugue et Variation, 136
Prière in C sharp, 136
Prix de Rome, 34
Procession, The, 78, 176
Psyche, dedication of, 173
    popular neglect of, 12
    spiritual character of, 78, 173–176
Puvis de Chavannes, 61, 65

Quæ est ista, 130
Quartet in D major, 54, 88, 144, 160, 171, 180

Quartet—continued
  composition of, 65, 184–
    189, 193
  diagram of, 192
  Finale, 194–197
  harmonious beauty of,
    analysed, 189-197
  Larghetto, 119, 193
  success of, 55, 56
Quartet, composition of, 182–
  184
Quasi Marcia, 127
Quincy, 64
Quintet in F minor, 88, 161, 189

RADOUX, Théodore, 210
Rameau, 18
Raphael Sanzio, 76
Ratisbonne, 80
Rebecca, 78, 161
Reber, Henri, 244
Reboul, Jean, *L'Ange et l'Enfant*,
  112
Récy, René de, on *The Beati-
  tudes*, 228
Redemption, 76, 78, 103, 127
  analysis of, 142, 145–151
  compared with *The Beati-
    tudes*, 216, 219, 221
  composition of, 47, 209
  first performance of, 47,
    151–154
  history of, 143, 151–158
  Liszt's delight in, 112
  plan of the poem, 144
  two versions of, 143, 149,
    151, 154–158
Reicha, Antoine, 114, 115
Reinecke, 183
Rembrandt, 30, 248
Rémy, M., 161
Renaissance, the, 174, 199
  cause of sterility of, 75, 128

Renan, Ernest, 69
  Life of Christ, 213
  Revue Bleue, La, 228 note
  Revue Internationale de Musique,
    159 note
Richault, M., 125, 126
Robert le Diable, 224
Roi d'Ys, Le, 172
Rolland, M. Romain, *Musiciens
  d'aujourdhui*, 8, 18
  on César Franck, 10
  on indifference to music
    under the Second Em-
    pire, 8, 9
  on the *Schola Cantorum*, 18
  on Vincent d'Indy, 15
Rongier, Mme. Jeanne, 63 note
Ropartz, J. Guy, on Franck,
    159, 254
  Symphonies Modernes, 173
Rossini, popularity of, 8
  Stabat mater, 153
Rouet d'Omphale, Le, 79
Rousseau, Samuel, 180 note, 251
Royer, Alphonse, 39, 40
Rubens, P. P., 76
Russia, National School of Art
  and Literature in, 9
Ruth, 78, 93, 102
  analysis of, 120–124
  criticisms of, 37, 38
  production of, 37, 52

SAINT-CHAMOND, 20
Saint-Jean-de-Luz, 20
Saint-Réné-Taillandier, G., 251
Saint-Saëns, M., 59 note, 67,
    161, 256
  arranges the *Prélude, Fugue
    et Variation*, 136
  C minor *Symphony*, 172,
    173 note
Cœli enarrant, 153

Saint-Saëns, M.—*continued*
  Franck's tribute to, 68
  Le Rouet d'Omphale, 79
Samson et Dalila, 68
San Gimignano, 176
Sano di Pietro, 76
Sauge-Fleurie, 15
Schiller, Friedrich, *Lay of the*
  Bell, 15
Schlésinger, M., 110, 117
Schola Cantorum, foundation of,
  17, 255 note
  progress of, 18–20
Schubert, Franz, 87, 253
  influence on Franck, 110
  Lieder, 94
  quartets of, 184
Schuberth & Co., 106
Schumann, Robert, 87, 94, 100,
  242, 253
  Faust, 204, 205
  writes for pianoforte, 162
Schütz, Heinrich, 18
  Dialogus per la Pascua, 212
  note, 221
Second empire, indifference to
  music during, 8
Serres, Louis de, 254
Sheffield Musical Festival, 12
Société Nationale de Musique,
  251
  activity of, 162
  concerts of, 112, 161, 164,
    168, 169 note, 173,
    176
  Franck president of, 55
  perform the *String Quartet*,
    56, 57
  tribute to Franck, 59
Société des Concerts, 251
Solo for Piano, Op. 10, 125
Sonata, renovation of the, 85,
  168

Sonata in A for Violin and Piano,
  54, 55, 88, 189
  analysis of, 169–171
Souvenir of Aix-la-Chapelle, 126
Spohr, 87
Stabat Mater, 153
St. Francis of Assisi, 174
Stratonice, 93
Strauss, Richard, 80
String Quartet—see *Quartet* in
  D major
Symphonic form, 172
Symphonie Cévenole, 15
  Fantastique, 87
Symphonies Modernes, 173 note
Symphony for Orchestra, 207
Symphony in D minor, 136, 189
  analysed, 171–173
  first performance of, 54
  influence of Beethoven in,
    95

Tannhäuser, 104
Thalberg, 35
Thomas, Ambrose, 59
Tournai, 56
Tournemire, Ch., 251
"Tranches de Vie," 248, 249
Trios concertans, trois, Op. 1, 102,
  161
  first trio in F sharp, 88, 93,
    105–109
  second trio, 109
  third trio, 110, 111
  dedication of, 36, 105
  influence of Beethoven in,
    105
  key of, 119
Trio concertant quatrième, Op. 2,
  93, 110
Trio de Salon, 110
Tristan, 104
Trois petit riens, Op. 16, 126

Trois pièces pour grand orgue, 161

Twelfth Quartet (Beethoven), 87

UTRECHT, 210

VÆS, Gustave 39
Valet de Ferme, Le, composition of, 40
Vallin, Gaston, 254
Van Dyck, 76
Variation-form, decline of, 85
Variations Symphoniques, 52, 53, 57, 169
Veuillot, Louis, 61
Viardot, Madame Pauline, 31
Paul, 112
Vidal, Paul, 251
Vierge à la Crèche, La, 78, 176
Violin Sonata—see *Sonata* in A
Viotta, Signor, 210
Vita Nuova, 206
Voyage en Chine, Le, 61

WAGNER, Richard, 89, 242
influence of, in France, 9, 11, 15
his use of *leitmotiv,* 225
influence on Franck, 37, 96, 134
Nibelungen, 204, 205
Wailly, Paul de, 254
Walküre, Die, 134
Wallenstein's Camp, 14
Weber, Charles, *Euryanthe,* 94
influence on Franck, 110, 117
Weimar, 111 note, 112
Wiertz, Antoine, 78
Wœfelghem, Van, 161
Wood, Mr. Henry J., 12

YSAYE, Eugène, plays the *Violin Sonata,* 12, 21, 55, 251
Sonata in A, dedicated to, 54, 170
Ysaye Quartet, the, 56
Ysaye, Théophile, 54

ZIMMERMANN, Peter, 31

A CATALOGUE OF SELECTED DOVER BOOKS
IN ALL FIELDS OF INTEREST

A CATALOGUE OF SELECTED DOVER BOOKS
IN ALL FIELDS OF INTEREST

WHAT IS SCIENCE?, *N. Campbell*
The role of experiment and measurement, the function of mathematics, the nature of scientific laws, the difference between laws and theories, the limitations of science, and many similarly provocative topics are treated clearly and without technicalities by an eminent scientist. "Still an excellent introduction to scientific philosophy," H. Margenau in *Physics Today*. "A first-rate primer . . . deserves a wide audience," *Scientific American*. 192pp. 5⅜ x 8.
60043-2 Paperbound $1.25

THE NATURE OF LIGHT AND COLOUR IN THE OPEN AIR, *M. Minnaert*
Why are shadows sometimes blue, sometimes green, or other colors depending on the light and surroundings? What causes mirages? Why do multiple suns and moons appear in the sky? Professor Minnaert explains these unusual phenomena and hundreds of others in simple, easy-to-understand terms based on optical laws and the properties of light and color. No mathematics is required but artists, scientists, students, and everyone fascinated by these "tricks" of nature will find thousands of useful and amazing pieces of information. Hundreds of observational experiments are suggested which require no special equipment. 200 illustrations; 42 photos. xvi + 362pp. 5⅜ x 8.
20196-1 Paperbound $2.00

THE STRANGE STORY OF THE QUANTUM, AN ACCOUNT FOR THE GENERAL READER OF THE GROWTH OF IDEAS UNDERLYING OUR PRESENT ATOMIC KNOWLEDGE, *B. Hoffmann*
Presents lucidly and expertly, with barest amount of mathematics, the problems and theories which led to modern quantum physics. Dr. Hoffmann begins with the closing years of the 19th century, when certain trifling discrepancies were noticed, and with illuminating analogies and examples takes you through the brilliant concepts of Planck, Einstein, Pauli, Broglie, Bohr, Schroedinger, Heisenberg, Dirac, Sommerfeld, Feynman, etc. This edition includes a new, long postscript carrying the story through 1958. "Of the books attempting an account of the history and contents of our modern atomic physics which have come to my attention, this is the best," H. Margenau, Yale University, in *American Journal of Physics*. 32 tables and line illustrations. Index. 275pp. 5⅜ x 8.
20518-5 Paperbound $2.00

GREAT IDEAS OF MODERN MATHEMATICS: THEIR NATURE AND USE, *Jagjit Singh*
Reader with only high school math will understand main mathematical ideas of modern physics, astronomy, genetics, psychology, evolution, etc. better than many who use them as tools, but comprehend little of their basic structure. Author uses his wide knowledge of non-mathematical fields in brilliant exposition of differential equations, matrices, group theory, logic, statistics, problems of mathematical foundations, imaginary numbers, vectors, etc. Original publication. 2 appendixes. 2 indexes. 65 ills. 322pp. 5⅜ x 8.
20587-8 Paperbound $2.25

FAIRY TALE COLLECTIONS, *edited by Andrew Lang*
Andrew Lang's fairy tale collections make up the richest shelf-full of traditional children's stories anywhere available. Lang supervised the translation of stories from all over the world—familiar European tales collected by Grimm, animal stories from Negro Africa, myths of primitive Australia, stories from Russia, Hungary, Iceland, Japan, and many other countries. Lang's selection of translations are unusually high; many authorities consider that the most familiar tales find their best versions in these volumes. All collections are richly decorated and illustrated by H. J. Ford and other artists.

THE BLUE FAIRY BOOK. 37 stories. 138 illustrations. ix + 390pp. 5⅜ x 8½.
21437-0 Paperbound $1.95

THE GREEN FAIRY BOOK. 42 stories. 100 illustrations. xiii + 366pp. 5⅜ x 8½.
21439-7 Paperbound $1.75

THE BROWN FAIRY BOOK. 32 stories. 50 illustrations, 8 in color. xii + 350pp. 5⅜ x 8½.
21438-9 Paperbound $1.95

THE BEST TALES OF HOFFMANN, *edited by E. F. Bleiler*
10 stories by E. T. A. Hoffmann, one of the greatest of all writers of fantasy. The tales include "The Golden Flower Pot," "Automata," "A New Year's Eve Adventure," "Nutcracker and the King of Mice," "Sand-Man," and others. Vigorous characterizations of highly eccentric personalities, remarkably imaginative situations, and intensely fast pacing has made these tales popular all over the world for 150 years. Editor's introduction. 7 drawings by Hoffmann. xxxiii + 419pp. 5⅜ x 8½.
21793-0 Paperbound $2.25

GHOST AND HORROR STORIES OF AMBROSE BIERCE, *edited by E. F. Bleiler*
Morbid, eerie, horrifying tales of possessed poets, shabby aristocrats, revived corpses, and haunted malefactors. Widely acknowledged as the best of their kind between Poe and the moderns, reflecting their author's inner torment and bitter view of life. Includes "Damned Thing," "The Middle Toe of the Right Foot," "The Eyes of the Panther," "Visions of the Night," "Moxon's Master," and over a dozen others. Editor's introduction. xxii + 199pp. 5⅜ x 8½.
20767-6 Paperbound $1.50

THREE GOTHIC NOVELS, *edited by E. F. Bleiler*
Originators of the still popular Gothic novel form, influential in ushering in early 19th-century Romanticism. Horace Walpole's *Castle of Otranto*, William Beckford's *Vathek*, John Polidori's *The Vampyre*, and a *Fragment* by Lord Byron are enjoyable as exciting reading or as documents in the history of English literature. Editor's introduction. xi + 291pp. 5⅜ x 8½.
21232-7 Paperbound $2.00

BEST GHOST STORIES OF LEFANU, *edited by E. F. Bleiler*
Though admired by such critics as V. S. Pritchett, Charles Dickens and Henry James, ghost stories by the Irish novelist Joseph Sheridan LeFanu have never become as widely known as his detective fiction. About half of the 16 stories in this collection have never before been available in America. Collection includes "Carmilla" (perhaps the best vampire story ever written), "The Haunted Baronet," "The Fortunes of Sir Robert Ardagh," and the classic "Green Tea." Editor's introduction. 7 contemporary illustrations. Portrait of LeFanu. xii + 467pp. 5⅜ x 8.
20415-4 Paperbound $2.50

THE RISE OF THE NEW PHYSICS (formerly THE DECLINE OF MECHANISM), *A. d'Abro*
This authoritative and comprehensive 2-volume exposition is unique in scientific publishing. Written for intelligent readers not familiar with higher mathematics, it is the only thorough explanation in non-technical language of modern mathematical-physical theory. Combining both history and exposition, it ranges from classical Newtonian concepts up through the electronic theories of Dirac and Heisenberg, the statistical mechanics of Fermi, and Einstein's relativity theories. "A must for anyone doing serious study in the physical sciences," *J. of Franklin Inst.* 97 illustrations. 991pp. 2 volumes.
20003-5, 20004-3 Two volume set, paperbound $5.50

THE STRANGE STORY OF THE QUANTUM, AN ACCOUNT FOR THE GENERAL READER OF THE GROWTH OF IDEAS UNDERLYING OUR PRESENT ATOMIC KNOWLEDGE, *B. Hoffmann*
Presents lucidly and expertly, with barest amount of mathematics, the problems and theories which led to modern quantum physics. Dr. Hoffmann begins with the closing years of the 19th century, when certain trifling discrepancies were noticed, and with illuminating analogies and examples takes you through the brilliant concepts of Planck, Einstein, Pauli, de Broglie, Bohr, Schroedinger, Heisenberg, Dirac, Sommerfeld, Feynman, etc. This edition includes a new, long postscript carrying the story through 1958. "Of the books attempting an account of the history and contents of our modern atomic physics which have come to my attention, this is the best," H. Margenau, Yale University, in *American Journal of Physics.* 32 tables and line illustrations. Index. 275pp. 5⅜ x 8.
20518-5 Paperbound $2.00

GREAT IDEAS AND THEORIES OF MODERN COSMOLOGY, *Jagjit Singh*
The theories of Jeans, Eddington, Milne, Kant, Bondi, Gold, Newton, Einstein, Gamow, Hoyle, Dirac, Kuiper, Hubble, Weizsäcker and many others on such cosmological questions as the origin of the universe, space and time, planet formation, "continuous creation," the birth, life, and death of the stars, the origin of the galaxies, etc. By the author of the popular *Great Ideas of Modern Mathematics.* A gifted popularizer of science, he makes the most difficult abstractions crystal-clear even to the most non-mathematical reader. Index. xii + 276pp. 5⅜ x 8½.
20925-3 Paperbound $2.50

GREAT IDEAS OF MODERN MATHEMATICS: THEIR NATURE AND USE, *Jagjit Singh*
Reader with only high school math will understand main mathematical ideas of modern physics, astronomy, genetics, psychology, evolution, etc., better than many who use them as tools, but comprehend little of their basic structure. Author uses his wide knowledge of non-mathematical fields in brilliant exposition of differential equations, matrices, group theory, logic, statistics, problems of mathematical foundations, imaginary numbers, vectors, etc. Original publications, appendices. indexes. 65 illustr. 322pp. 5⅜ x 8. 20587-8 Paperbound $2.25

THE MATHEMATICS OF GREAT AMATEURS, *Julian L. Coolidge*
Great discoveries made by poets, theologians, philosophers, artists and other non-mathematicians: Omar Khayyam, Leonardo da Vinci, Albrecht Dürer, John Napier, Pascal, Diderot, Bolzano, etc. Surprising accounts of what can result from a non-professional preoccupation with the oldest of sciences. 56 figures. viii + 211pp. 5⅜ x 8½.
61009-8 Paperbound $2.00

THE MUSIC OF THE SPHERES: THE MATERIAL UNIVERSE — FROM ATOM TO QUASAR, SIMPLY EXPLAINED, *Guy Murchie*
Vast compendium of fact, modern concept and theory, observed and calculated data, historical background guides intelligent layman through the material universe. Brilliant exposition of earth's construction, explanations for moon's craters, atmospheric components of Venus and Mars (with data from recent fly-by's), sun spots, sequences of star birth and death, neighboring galaxies, contributions of Galileo, Tycho Brahe, Kepler, etc.; and (Vol. 2) construction of the atom (describing newly discovered sigma and xi subatomic particles), theories of sound, color and light, space and time, including relativity theory, quantum theory, wave theory, probability theory, work of Newton, Maxwell, Faraday, Einstein, de Broglie, etc. "Best presentation yet offered to the intelligent general reader," *Saturday Review*. Revised (1967). Index. 319 illustrations by the author. Total of xx + 644pp. 5⅜ x 8½.
21809-0, 21810-4   Two volume set, paperbound $5.00

FOUR LECTURES ON RELATIVITY AND SPACE, *Charles Proteus Steinmetz*
Lecture series, given by great mathematician and electrical engineer, generally considered one of the best popular-level expositions of special and general relativity theories and related questions. Steinmetz translates complex mathematical reasoning into language accessible to laymen through analogy, example and comparison. Among topics covered are relativity of motion, location, time; of mass; acceleration; 4-dimensional time-space; geometry of the gravitational field; curvature and bending of space; non-Euclidean geometry. Index. 40 illustrations. x + 142pp. 5⅜ x 8½.
61771-8 Paperbound $1.35

HOW TO KNOW THE WILD FLOWERS, *Mrs. William Starr Dana*
Classic nature book that has introduced thousands to wonders of American wild flowers. Color-season principle of organization is easy to use, even by those with no botanical training, and the genial, refreshing discussions of history, folklore, uses of over 1,000 native and escape flowers, foliage plants are informative as well as fun to read. Over 170 full-page plates, collected from several editions, may be colored in to make permanent records of finds. Revised to conform with 1950 edition of Gray's Manual of Botany. xlii + 438pp. 5⅜ x 8½.
20332-8 Paperbound $2.50

MANUAL OF THE TREES OF NORTH AMERICA, *Charles Sprague Sargent*
Still unsurpassed as most comprehensive, reliable study of North American tree characteristics, precise locations and distribution. By dean of American dendrologists. Every tree native to U.S., Canada, Alaska; 185 genera, 717 species, described in detail—leaves, flowers, fruit, winterbuds, bark, wood, growth habits, etc. plus discussion of varieties and local variants, immaturity variations. Over 100 keys, including unusual 11-page analytical key to genera, aid in identification. 783 clear illustrations of flowers, fruit, leaves. An unmatched permanent reference work for all nature lovers. Second enlarged (1926) edition. Synopsis of families. Analytical key to genera. Glossary of technical terms. Index. 783 illustrations, 1 map. Total of 982pp. 5⅜ x 8.
20277-1, 20278-X Two volume set, paperbound $6.00

PRINCIPLES OF ART HISTORY,
H. Wölfflin
Analyzing such terms as "baroque," "classic," "neoclassic," "primitive," "picturesque," and 164 different works by artists like Botticelli, van Cleve, Dürer, Hobbema, Holbein, Hals, Rembrandt, Titian, Brueghel, Vermeer, and many others, the author establishes the classifications of art history and style on a firm, concrete basis. This classic of art criticism shows what really occurred between the 14th-century primitives and the sophistication of the 18th century in terms of basic attitudes and philosophies. "A remarkable lesson in the art of seeing," *Sat. Rev. of Literature.* Translated from the 7th German edition. 150 illustrations. 254pp. 6⅛ x 9¼. 20276-3 Paperbound $2.25

PRIMITIVE ART,
Franz Boas
This authoritative and exhaustive work by a great American anthropologist covers the entire gamut of primitive art. Pottery, leatherwork, metal work, stone work, wood, basketry, are treated in detail. Theories of primitive art, historical depth in art history, technical virtuosity, unconscious levels of patterning, symbolism, styles, literature, music, dance, etc. A must book for the interested layman, the anthropologist, artist, handicrafter (hundreds of unusual motifs), and the historian. Over 900 illustrations (50 ceramic vessels, 12 totem poles, etc.). 376pp. 5⅜ x 8. 20025-6 Paperbound $2.50

THE GENTLEMAN AND CABINET MAKER'S DIRECTOR,
Thomas Chippendale
A reprint of the 1762 catalogue of furniture designs that went on to influence generations of English and Colonial and Early Republic American furniture makers. The 200 plates, most of them full-page sized, show Chippendale's designs for French (Louis XV), Gothic, and Chinese-manner chairs, sofas, canopy and dome beds, cornices, chamber organs, cabinets, shaving tables, commodes, picture frames, frets, candle stands, chimney pieces, decorations, etc. The drawings are all elegant and highly detailed; many include construction diagrams and elevations. A supplement of 24 photographs shows surviving pieces of original and Chippendale-style pieces of furniture. Brief biography of Chippendale by N. I. Bienenstock, editor of *Furniture World.* Reproduced from the 1762 edition. 200 plates, plus 19 photographic plates. vi + 249pp. 9⅛ x 12¼. 21601-2 Paperbound $3.50

AMERICAN ANTIQUE FURNITURE: A BOOK FOR AMATEURS,
Edgar G. Miller, Jr.
Standard introduction and practical guide to identification of valuable American antique furniture. 2115 illustrations, mostly photographs taken by the author in 148 private homes, are arranged in chronological order in extensive chapters on chairs, sofas, chests, desks, bedsteads, mirrors, tables, clocks, and other articles. Focus is on furniture accessible to the collector, including simpler pieces and a larger than usual coverage of Empire style. Introductory chapters identify structural elements, characteristics of various styles, how to avoid fakes, etc. "We are frequently asked to name some book on American furniture that will meet the requirements of the novice collector, the beginning dealer, and . . . the general public. . . . We believe Mr. Miller's two volumes more completely satisfy this specification than any other work," *Antiques.* Appendix. Index. Total of vi + 1106pp. 7⅞ x 10¾. 21599-7, 21600-4 Two volume set, paperbound $7.50

AN INTRODUCTION TO THE GEOMETRY OF N DIMENSIONS,
D. H. Y. Sommerville
An introduction presupposing no prior knowledge of the field, the only book
in English devoted exclusively to higher dimensional geometry. Discusses
fundamental ideas of incidence, parallelism, perpendicularity, angles between
linear space; enumerative geometry; analytical geometry from projective and
metric points of view; polytopes; elementary ideas in analysis situs; content of
hyper-spacial figures. Bibliography. Index. 60 diagrams. 196pp. 5⅜ x 8.
60494-2 Paperbound $1.50

ELEMENTARY CONCEPTS OF TOPOLOGY, *P. Alexandroff*
First English translation of the famous brief introduction to topology for the
beginner or for the mathematician not undertaking extensive study. This unusually useful intuitive approach deals primarily with the concepts of complex,
cycle, and homology, and is wholly consistent with current investigations.
Ranges from basic concepts of set-theoretic topology to the concept of Betti
groups. "Glowing example of harmony between intuition and thought," David
Hilbert. Translated by A. E. Farley. Introduction by D. Hilbert. Index. 25
figures. 73pp. 5⅜ x 8.   60747-X Paperbound $1.25

ELEMENTS OF NON-EUCLIDEAN GEOMETRY,
D. M. Y. Sommerville
Unique in proceeding step-by-step, in the manner of traditional geometry.
Enables the student with only a good knowledge of high school algebra and
geometry to grasp elementary hyperbolic, elliptic, analytic non-Euclidean geom-
etries; space curvature and its philosophical implications; theory of radical
axes; homothetic centres and systems of circles; parataxy and parallelism;
absolute measure; Gauss' proof of the defect area theorem; geodesic representation; much more, all with exceptional clarity. 126 problems at chapter endings
provide progressive practice and familiarity. 133 figures. Index. xvi + 274pp.
5⅜ x 8.   60460-8 Paperbound $2.00

INTRODUCTION TO THE THEORY OF NUMBERS, *L. E. Dickson*
Thorough, comprehensive approach with adequate coverage of classical literature, an introductory volume beginners can follow. Chapters on divisibility,
congruences, quadratic residues & reciprocity. Diophantine equations, etc. Full
treatment of binary quadratic forms without usual restriction to integral coefficients. Covers infinitude of primes, least residues. Fermat's theorem. Euler's
phi function, Legendre's symbol, Gauss's lemma, automorphs, reduced forms,
recent theorems of Thue & Siegel, many more. Much material not readily
available elsewhere. 239 problems. Index. I figure. viii + 183pp. 5⅜ x 8.
60342-3 Paperbound $1.75

MATHEMATICAL TABLES AND FORMULAS,
compiled by Robert D. Carmichael and Edwin R. Smith
Valuable collection for students, etc. Contains all tables necessary in college
algebra and trigonometry, such as five-place common logarithms, logarithmic
sines and tangents of small angles, logarithmic trigonometric functions, natural
trigonometric functions, four-place antilogarithms, tables for changing from
sexagesimal to circular and from circular to sexagesimal measure of angles, etc.
Also many tables and formulas not ordinarily accessible, including powers,
roots, and reciprocals, exponential and hyperbolic functions, ten-place logarithms of prime numbers, and formulas and theorems from analytical and
elementary geometry and from calculus. Explanatory introduction. viii +
269pp. 5⅜ x 8½.   60111-0 Paperbound $1.50

CHANCE, LUCK AND STATISTICS: THE SCIENCE OF CHANCE,
Horace C. Levinson
Theory of probability and science of statistics in simple, non-technical language. Part I deals with theory of probability, covering odd superstitions in regard to "luck," the meaning of betting odds, the law of mathematical expectation, gambling, and applications in poker, roulette, lotteries, dice, bridge, and other games of chance. Part II discusses the misuse of statistics, the concept of statistical probabilities, normal and skew frequency distributions, and statistics applied to various fields—birth rates, stock speculation, insurance rates, advertising, etc. "Presented in an easy humorous style which I consider the best kind of expository writing," Prof. A. C. Cohen, Industry Quality Control. Enlarged revised edition. Formerly titled *The Science of Chance*. Preface and two new appendices by the author. xiv + 365pp. 5⅜ x 8. 21007-3 Paperbound $2.00

BASIC ELECTRONICS,
prepared by the U.S. Navy Training Publications Center
A thorough and comprehensive manual on the fundamentals of electronics. Written clearly, it is equally useful for self-study or course work for those with a knowledge of the principles of basic electricity. Partial contents: Operating Principles of the Electron Tube; Introduction to Transistors; Power Supplies for Electronic Equipment; Tuned Circuits; Electron-Tube Amplifiers; Audio Power Amplifiers; Oscillators; Transmitters; Transmission Lines; Antennas and Propagation; Introduction to Computers; and related topics. Appendix. Index. Hundreds of illustrations and diagrams. vi + 471pp. 6½ x 9¼.
61076-4 Paperbound $2.95

BASIC THEORY AND APPLICATION OF TRANSISTORS,
prepared by the U.S. Department of the Army
An introductory manual prepared for an army training program. One of the finest available surveys of theory and application of transistor design and operation. Minimal knowledge of physics and theory of electron tubes required. Suitable for textbook use, course supplement, or home study. Chapters: Introduction; fundamental theory of transistors; transistor amplifier fundamentals; parameters, equivalent circuits, and characteristic curves; bias stabilization; transistor analysis and comparison using characteristic curves and charts; audio amplifiers; tuned amplifiers; wide-band amplifiers; oscillators; pulse and switching circuits; modulation, mixing, and demodulation; and additional semiconductor devices. Unabridged, corrected edition. 240 schematic drawings, photographs, wiring diagrams, etc. 2 Appendices. Glossary. Index. 263pp. 6½ x 9¼.
60380-6 Paperbound $1.75

GUIDE TO THE LITERATURE OF MATHEMATICS AND PHYSICS,
N. G. Parke III
Over 5000 entries included under approximately 120 major subject headings of selected most important books, monographs, periodicals, articles in English, plus important works in German, French, Italian, Spanish, Russian (many recently available works). Covers every branch of physics, math, related engineering. Includes author, title, edition, publisher, place, date, number of volumes, number of pages. A 40-page introduction on the basic problems of research and study provides useful information on the organization and use of libraries, the psychology of learning, etc. This reference work will save you hours of time. 2nd revised edition. Indices of authors, subjects, 464pp. 5⅜ x 8.
60447-0 Paperbound $2.75

THE PRINCIPLES OF PSYCHOLOGY,
William James
The full long-course, unabridged, of one of the great classics of Western literature and science. Wonderfully lucid descriptions of human mental activity, the stream of thought, consciousness, time perception, memory, imagination, emotions, reason, abnormal phenomena, and similar topics. Original contributions are integrated with the work of such men as Berkeley, Binet, Mills, Darwin, Hume, Kant, Royce, Schopenhauer, Spinoza, Locke, Descartes, Galton, Wundt, Lotze, Herbart, Fechner, and scores of others. All contrasting interpretations of mental phenomena are examined in detail—introspective analysis, philosophical interpretation, and experimental research. "A classic," *Journal of Consulting Psychology*. "The main lines are as valid as ever," *Psychoanalytical Quarterly*. "Standard reading ... a classic of interpretation," *Psychiatric Quarterly*. 94 illustrations. 1408pp. 5⅜ x 8.
20381-6, 20382-4 Two volume set, paperbound $6.00

VISUAL ILLUSIONS: THEIR CAUSES, CHARACTERISTICS AND APPLICATIONS,
M. Luckiesh
"Seeing is deceiving," asserts the author of this introduction to virtually every type of optical illusion known. The text both describes and explains the principles involved in color illusions, figure-ground, distance illusions, etc. 100 photographs, drawings and diagrams prove how easy it is to fool the sense: circles that aren't round, parallel lines that seem to bend, stationary figures that seem to move as you stare at them — illustration after illustration strains our credulity at what we see. Fascinating book from many points of view, from applications for artists, in camouflage, etc. to the psychology of vision. New introduction by William Ittleson, Dept. of Psychology, Queens College. Index. Bibliography. xxi + 252pp. 5⅜ x 8½.
21530-X Paperbound $1.50

FADS AND FALLACIES IN THE NAME OF SCIENCE,
Martin Gardner
This is the standard account of various cults, quack systems, and delusions which have masqueraded as science: hollow earth fanatics. Reich and orgone sex energy, dianetics, Atlantis, multiple moons, Forteanism, flying saucers, medical fallacies like iridiagnosis, zone therapy, etc. A new chapter has been added on Bridey Murphy, psionics, and other recent manifestations in this field. This is a fair, reasoned appraisal of eccentric theory which provides excellent inoculation against cleverly masked nonsense. "Should be read by everyone, scientist and non-scientist alike," R. T. Birge, Prof. Emeritus of Physics, Univ. of California; Former President, American Physical Society. Index. x + 365pp. 5⅜ x 8.
20394-8 Paperbound $2.00

ILLUSIONS AND DELUSIONS OF THE SUPERNATURAL AND THE OCCULT,
D. H. Rawcliffe
Holds up to rational examination hundreds of persistent delusions including crystal gazing, automatic writing, table turning, mediumistic trances, mental healing, stigmata, lycanthropy, live burial, the Indian Rope Trick, spiritualism, dowsing, telepathy, clairvoyance, ghosts, ESP, etc. The author explains and exposes the mental and physical deceptions involved, making this not only an exposé of supernatural phenomena, but a valuable exposition of characteristic types of abnormal psychology. Originally titled "The Psychology of the Occult." 14 illustrations. Index. 551pp. 5⅜ x 8. 20503-7 Paperbound $3.50

SOCIAL THOUGHT FROM LORE TO SCIENCE,
H. E. Barnes and H. Becker
An immense survey of sociological thought and ways of viewing, studying, planning, and reforming society from earliest times to the present. Includes thought on society of preliterate peoples, ancient non-Western cultures, and every great movement in Europe, America, and modern Japan. Analyzes hundreds of great thinkers: Plato, Augustine, Bodin, Vico, Montesquieu, Herder, Comte, Marx, etc. Weighs the contributions of utopians, sophists, fascists and communists; economists, jurists, philosophers, ecclesiastics, and every 19th and 20th century school of scientific sociology, anthropology, and social psychology throughout the world. Combines topical, chronological, and regional approaches, treating the evolution of social thought as a process rather than as a series of mere topics. "Impressive accuracy, competence, and discrimination . . . easily the best single survey," *Nation*. Thoroughly revised, with new material up to 1960. 2 indexes. Over 2200 bibliographical notes. Three volume set. Total of 1586pp. 5⅜ x 8.
20901-6, 20902-4, 20903-2 Three volume set, paperbound $9.00

A HISTORY OF HISTORICAL WRITING, *Harry Elmer Barnes*
Virtually the only adequate survey of the whole course of historical writing in a single volume. Surveys developments from the beginnings of historiography in the ancient Near East and the Classical World, up through the Cold War. Covers major historians in detail, shows interrelationship with cultural background, makes clear individual contributions, evaluates and estimates importance; also enormously rich upon minor authors and thinkers who are usually passed over. Packed with scholarship and learning, clear, easily written. Indispensable to every student of history. Revised and enlarged up to 1961. Index and bibliography. xv + 442pp. 5⅜ x 8½.
20104-X Paperbound $2.75

JOHANN SEBASTIAN BACH, *Philipp Spitta*
The complete and unabridged text of the definitive study of Bach. Written some 70 years ago, it is still unsurpassed for its coverage of nearly all aspects of Bach's life and work. There could hardly be a finer non-technical introduction to Bach's music than the detailed, lucid analyses which Spitta provides for hundreds of individual pieces. 26 solid pages are devoted to the B minor mass, for example, and 30 pages to the glorious St. Matthew Passion. This monumental set also includes a major analysis of the music of the 18th century: Buxtehude, Pachelbel, etc. "Unchallenged as the last word on one of the supreme geniuses of music," John Barkham, *Saturday Review Syndicate*. Total of 1819pp. Heavy cloth binding. 5⅜ x 8.
22278-0, 22279-9 Two volume set, clothbound $15.00

BEETHOVEN AND HIS NINE SYMPHONIES, *George Grove*
In this modern middle-level classic of musicology Grove not only analyzes all nine of Beethoven's symphonies very thoroughly in terms of their musical structure, but also discusses the circumstances under which they were written, Beethoven's stylistic development, and much other background material. This is an extremely rich book, yet very easily followed; it is highly recommended to anyone seriously interested in music. Over 250 musical passages. Index. viii + 407pp. 5⅜ x 8.
20334-4 Paperbound $2.25

COLLEGE ALGEBRA, *H. B. Fine*
Standard college text that gives a systematic and deductive structure to algebra; comprehensive, connected, with emphasis on theory. Discusses the commutative, associative, and distributive laws of number in unusual detail, and goes on with undetermined coefficients, quadratic equations, progressions, logarithms, permutations, probability, power series, and much more. Still most valuable elementary-intermediate text on the science and structure of algebra. Index. 1560 problems, all with answers. x + 631pp. 5⅜ x 8. 60211-7 Paperbound $2.75

HIGHER MATHEMATICS FOR STUDENTS OF CHEMISTRY AND PHYSICS, *J. W. Mellor*
Not abstract, but practical, building its problems out of familiar laboratory material, this covers differential calculus, coordinate, analytical geometry, functions, integral calculus, infinite series, numerical equations, differential equations, Fourier's theorem, probability, theory of errors, calculus of variations, determinants. "If the reader is not familiar with this book, it will repay him to examine it," *Chem. & Engineering News.* 800 problems. 189 figures. Bibliography. xxi + 641pp. 5⅜ x 8. 60193-5 Paperbound $3.50

TRIGONOMETRY REFRESHER FOR TECHNICAL MEN, *A. A. Klaf*
A modern question and answer text on plane and spherical trigonometry. Part I covers plane trigonometry: angles, quadrants, trigonometrical functions, graphical representation, interpolation, equations, logarithms, solution of triangles, slide rules, etc. Part II discusses applications to navigation, surveying, elasticity, architecture, and engineering. Small angles, periodic functions, vectors, polar coordinates, De Moivre's theorem, fully covered. Part III is devoted to spherical trigonometry and the solution of spherical triangles, with applications to terrestrial and astronomical problems. Special time-savers for numerical calculation. 913 questions answered for you! 1738 problems; answers to odd numbers. 494 figures. 14 pages of functions, formulae. Index. x + 629pp. 5⅜ x 8. 20371-9 Paperbound $3.00

CALCULUS REFRESHER FOR TECHNICAL MEN, *A. A. Klaf*
Not an ordinary textbook but a unique refresher for engineers, technicians, and students. An examination of the most important aspects of differential and integral calculus by means of 756 key questions. Part I covers simple differential calculus: constants, variables, functions, increments, derivatives, logarithms, curvature, etc. Part II treats fundamental concepts of integration: inspection, substitution, transformation, reduction, areas and volumes, mean value, successive and partial integration, double and triple integration. Stresses practical aspects! A 50 page section gives applications to civil and nautical engineering, electricity, stress and strain, elasticity, industrial engineering, and similar fields. 756 questions answered. 556 problems; solutions to odd numbers. 36 pages of constants, formulae. Index. v + 431pp. 5⅜ x 8. 20370-0 Paperbound $2.25

INTRODUCTION TO THE THEORY OF GROUPS OF FINITE ORDER, *R. Carmichael*
Examines fundamental theorems and their application. Beginning with sets, systems, permutations, etc., it progresses in easy stages through important types of groups: Abelian, prime power, permutation, etc. Except 1 chapter where matrices are desirable, no higher math needed. 783 exercises, problems. Index. xvi + 447pp. 5⅜ x 8. 60300-8 Paperbound $3.00

EASY-TO-DO ENTERTAINMENTS AND DIVERSIONS WITH COINS, CARDS, STRING, PAPER AND MATCHES, R. M. Abraham
Over 300 tricks, games and puzzles will provide young readers with absorbing fun. Sections on card games; paper-folding; tricks with coins, matches and pieces of string; games for the agile; toy-making from common household objects; mathematical recreations; and 50 miscellaneous pastimes. Anyone in charge of groups of youngsters, including hard-pressed parents, and in need of suggestions on how to keep children sensibly amused and quietly content will find this book indispensable. Clear, simple text, copious number of delightful line drawings and illustrative diagrams. Originally titled "Winter Nights' Entertainments." Introduction by Lord Baden Powell. 329 illustrations. v + 186pp. 5⅜ x 8½.   20921-0 Paperbound $1.00

AN INTRODUCTION TO CHESS MOVES AND TACTICS SIMPLY EXPLAINED, Leonard Barden
Beginner's introduction to the royal game. Names, possible moves of the pieces, definitions of essential terms, how games are won, etc. explained in 30-odd pages. With this background you'll be able to sit right down and play. Balance of book teaches strategy — openings, middle game, typical endgame play, and suggestions for improving your game. A sample game is fully analyzed. True middle-level introduction, teaching you all the essentials without oversimplifying or losing you in a maze of detail. 58 figures. 102pp. 5⅜ x 8½.   21210-6 Paperbound $1.25

LASKER'S MANUAL OF CHESS, Dr. Emanuel Lasker
Probably the greatest chess player of modern times, Dr. Emanuel Lasker held the world championship 28 years, independent of passing schools or fashions. This unmatched study of the game, chiefly for intermediate to skilled players, analyzes basic methods, combinations, position play, the aesthetics of chess, dozens of different openings, etc., with constant reference to great modern games. Contains a brilliant exposition of Steinitz's important theories. Introduction by Fred Reinfeld. Tables of Lasker's tournament record. 3 indices. 308 diagrams. 1 photograph. xxx + 349pp. 5⅜ x 8.20640-8 Paperbound $2.50

COMBINATIONS: THE HEART OF CHESS, Irving Chernev
Step-by-step from simple combinations to complex, this book, by a well-known chess writer, shows you the intricacies of pins, counter-pins, knight forks, and smothered mates. Other chapters show alternate lines of play to those taken in actual championship games; boomerang combinations; classic examples of brilliant combination play by Nimzovich, Rubinstein, Tarrasch, Botvinnik, Alekhine and Capablanca. Index. 356 diagrams. ix + 245pp. 5⅜ x 8½.   21744-2 Paperbound $2.00

HOW TO SOLVE CHESS PROBLEMS, K. S. Howard
Full of practical suggestions for the fan or the beginner — who knows only the moves of the chessmen. Contains preliminary section and 58 two-move, 46 three-move, and 8 four-move problems composed by 27 outstanding American problem creators in the last 30 years. Explanation of all terms and exhaustive index. "Just what is wanted for the student," Brian Harley. 112 problems, solutions. vi + 171pp. 5⅜ x 8.   20748-X Paperbound $1.50

THE METHODS OF ETHICS, *Henry Sidgwick*
Propounding no organized system of its own, study subjects every major methodological approach to ethics to rigorous, objective analysis. Study discusses and relates ethical thought of Plato, Aristotle, Bentham, Clarke, Butler, Hobbes, Hume, Mill, Spencer, Kant, and dozens of others. Sidgwick retains conclusions from each system which follow from ethical premises, rejecting the faulty. Considered by many in the field to be among the most important treatises on ethical philosophy. Appendix. Index. xlvii + 528pp. 5⅜ x 8½.
21608-X Paperbound $2.50

TEUTONIC MYTHOLOGY, *Jakob Grimm*
A milestone in Western culture; the work which established on a modern basis the study of history of religions and comparative religions. 4-volume work assembles and interprets everything available on religious and folkloristic beliefs of Germanic people (including Scandinavians, Anglo-Saxons, etc.). Assembling material from such sources as Tacitus, surviving Old Norse and Icelandic texts, archeological remains, folktales, surviving superstitions, comparative traditions, linguistic analysis, etc. Grimm explores pagan deities, heroes, folklore of nature, religious practices, and every other area of pagan German belief. To this day, the unrivaled, definitive, exhaustive study. Translated by J. S. Stallybrass from 4th (1883) German edition. Indexes. Total of lxxvii + 1887pp. 5⅜ x 8½.
21602-0, 21603-9, 21604-7, 21605-5 Four volume set, paperbound $11.00

THE I CHING, *translated by James Legge*
Called "The Book of Changes" in English, this is one of the Five Classics edited by Confucius, basic and central to Chinese thought. Explains perhaps the most complex system of divination known, founded on the theory that all things happening at any one time have characteristic features which can be isolated and related. Significant in Oriental studies, in history of religions and philosophy, and also to Jungian psychoanalysis and other areas of modern European thought. Index. Appendixes. 6 plates. xxi + 448pp. 5⅜ x 8½.
21062-6 Paperbound $2.75

HISTORY OF ANCIENT PHILOSOPHY, *W. Windelband*
One of the clearest, most accurate comprehensive surveys of Greek and Roman philosophy. Discusses ancient philosophy in general, intellectual life in Greece in the 7th and 6th centuries B.C., Thales, Anaximander, Anaximenes, Heraclitus, the Eleatics, Empedocles, Anaxagoras, Leucippus, the Pythagoreans, the Sophists, Socrates, Democritus (20 pages), Plato (50 pages), Aristotle (70 pages), the Peripatetics, Stoics, Epicureans, Sceptics, Neo-platonists, Christian Apologists, etc. 2nd German edition translated by H. E. Cushman. xv + 393pp. 5⅜ x 8.
20357-3 Paperbound $2.25

THE PALACE OF PLEASURE, *William Painter*
Elizabethan versions of Italian and French novels from *The Decameron*, Cinthio, Straparola, Queen Margaret of Navarre, and other continental sources — the very work that provided Shakespeare and dozens of his contemporaries with many of their plots and sub-plots and, therefore, justly considered one of the most influential books in all English literature. It is also a book that any reader will still enjoy. Total of cviii + 1,224pp.
21691-8, 21692-6, 21693-4 Three volume set, paperbound $6.75

THREE SCIENCE FICTION NOVELS,
John Taine
Acknowledged by many as the best SF writer of the 1920's, Taine (under the name Eric Temple Bell) was also a Professor of Mathematics of considerable renown. Reprinted here are *The Time Stream*, generally considered Taine's best, *The Greatest Game*, a biological-fiction novel, and *The Purple Sapphire*, involving a supercivilization of the past. Taine's stories tie fantastic narratives to frameworks of original and logical scientific concepts. Speculation is often profound on such questions as the nature of time, concept of entropy, cyclical universes, etc. 4 contemporary illustrations. v + 532pp. 5⅜ x 8⅜.

21180-0 Paperbound $2.50

SEVEN SCIENCE FICTION NOVELS,
H. G. Wells
Full unabridged texts of 7 science-fiction novels of the master. Ranging from biology, physics, chemistry, astronomy, to sociology and other studies, Mr. Wells extrapolates whole worlds of strange and intriguing character. "One will have to go far to match this for entertainment, excitement, and sheer pleasure . . ."*New York Times*. Contents: The Time Machine, The Island of Dr. Moreau, The First Men in the Moon, The Invisible Man, The War of the Worlds, The Food of the Gods, In The Days of the Comet. 1015pp. 5⅜ x 8.

20264-X Clothbound $5.00

28 SCIENCE FICTION STORIES OF H. G. WELLS.
Two full, unabridged novels, *Men Like Gods* and *Star Begotten*, plus 26 short stories by the master science-fiction writer of all time! Stories of space, time, invention, exploration, futuristic adventure. Partial contents: *The Country of the Blind, In the Abyss, The Crystal Egg, The Man Who Could Work Miracles, A Story of Days to Come, The Empire of the Ants, The Magic Shop, The Valley of the Spiders, A Story of the Stone Age, Under the Knife, Sea Raiders*, etc. An indispensable collection for the library of anyone interested in science fiction adventure. 928pp. 5⅜ x 8.

20265-8 Clothbound $5.00

THREE MARTIAN NOVELS,
Edgar Rice Burroughs
Complete, unabridged reprinting, in one volume, of Thuvia, Maid of Mars; Chessmen of Mars; The Master Mind of Mars. Hours of science-fiction adventure by a modern master storyteller. Reset in large clear type for easy reading. 16 illustrations by J. Allen St. John. vi + 490pp. 5⅜ x 8½.

20039-6 Paperbound $2.50

AN INTELLECTUAL AND CULTURAL HISTORY OF THE WESTERN WORLD,
Harry Elmer Barnes
Monumental 3-volume survey of intellectual development of Europe from primitive cultures to the present day. Every significant product of human intellect traced through history: art, literature, mathematics, physical sciences, medicine, music, technology, social sciences, religions, jurisprudence, education, etc. Presentation is lucid and specific, analyzing in detail specific discoveries, theories, literary works, and so on. Revised (1965) by recognized scholars in specialized fields under the direction of Prof. Barnes. Revised bibliography. Indexes. 24 illustrations. Total of xxix + 1318pp.

21275-0, 21276-9, 21277-7 Three volume set, paperbound $8.25

HEAR ME TALKIN' TO YA, *edited by Nat Shapiro and Nat Hentoff*
In their own words, Louis Armstrong, King Oliver, Fletcher Henderson, Bunk Johnson, Bix Beiderbecke, Billy Holiday, Fats Waller, Jelly Roll Morton, Duke Ellington, and many others comment on the origins of jazz in New Orleans and its growth in Chicago's South Side, Kansas City's jam sessions, Depression Harlem, and the modernism of the West Coast schools. Taken from taped conversations, letters, magazine articles, other first-hand sources. Editors' introduction. xvi + 429pp. 5⅜ x 8½.   21726-4 Paperbound $2.00

THE JOURNAL OF HENRY D. THOREAU
A 25-year record by the great American observer and critic, as complete a record of a great man's inner life as is anywhere available. Thoreau's Journals served him as raw material for his formal pieces, as a place where he could develop his ideas, as an outlet for his interests in wild life and plants, in writing as an art, in classics of literature, Walt Whitman and other contemporaries, in politics, slavery, individual's relation to the State, etc. The Journals present a portrait of a remarkable man, and are an observant social history. Unabridged republication of 1906 edition, Bradford Torrey and Francis H. Allen, editors. Illustrations. Total of 1888pp. 8⅜ x 12¼.
20312-3, 20313-1 Two volume set. clothbound $30.00

A SHAKESPEARIAN GRAMMAR, *E. A. Abbott*
Basic reference to Shakespeare and his contemporaries, explaining through thousands of quotations from Shakespeare, Jonson, Beaumont and Fletcher, North's *Plutarch* and other sources the grammatical usage differing from the modern. First published in 1870 and written by a scholar who spent much of his life isolating principles of Elizabethan language, the book is unlikely ever to be superseded. Indexes. xxiv + 511pp. 5⅜ x 8½. 21582-2 Paperbound $3.00

FOLK-LORE OF SHAKESPEARE, *T. F. Thistelton Dyer*
Classic study, drawing from Shakespeare a large body of references to supernatural beliefs, terminology of falconry and hunting, games and sports, good luck charms, marriage customs, folk medicines, superstitions about plants, animals, birds, argot of the underworld, sexual slang of London, proverbs, drinking customs, weather lore, and much else. From full compilation comes a mirror of the 17th-century popular mind. Index. ix + 526pp. 5⅜ x 8½.
21614-4 Paperbound $2.75

THE NEW VARIORUM SHAKESPEARE, *edited by H. H. Furness*
By far the richest editions of the plays ever produced in any country or language. Each volume contains complete text (usually First Folio) of the play, all variants in Quarto and other Folio texts, editorial changes by every major editor to Furness's own time (1900), footnotes to obscure references or language, extensive quotes from literature of Shakespearian criticism, essays on plot sources (often reprinting sources in full), and much more.

HAMLET, *edited by H. H. Furness*
Total of xxvi + 905pp. 5⅜ x 8½.
21004-9, 21005-7 Two volume set, paperbound $5.25

TWELFTH NIGHT, *edited by H. H. Furness*
Index. xxii + 434pp. 5⅜ x 8½.   21189-4 Paperbound $2.75

IT'S FUN TO MAKE THINGS FROM SCRAP MATERIALS,
Evelyn Glantz Hershoff
What use are empty spools, tin cans, bottle tops? What can be made from rubber bands, clothes pins, paper clips, and buttons? This book provides simply worded instructions and large diagrams showing you how to make cookie cutters, toy trucks, paper turkeys, Halloween masks, telephone sets, aprons, linoleum block- and spatter prints — in all 399 projects! Many are easy enough for young children to figure out for themselves; some challenging enough to entertain adults; all are remarkably ingenious ways to make things from materials that cost pennies or less! Formerly "Scrap Fun for Everyone." Index. 214 illustrations. 373pp. 5⅜ x 8½.   21251-3 Paperbound $1.75

SYMBOLIC LOGIC and THE GAME OF LOGIC, *Lewis Carroll*
"Symbolic Logic" is not concerned with modern symbolic logic, but is instead a collection of over 380 problems posed with charm and imagination, using the syllogism and a fascinating diagrammatic method of drawing conclusions. In "The Game of Logic" Carroll's whimsical imagination devises a logical game played with 2 diagrams and counters (included) to manipulate hundreds of tricky syllogisms. The final section, "Hit or Miss" is a lagniappe of 101 additional puzzles in the delightful Carroll manner. Until this reprint edition, both of these books were rarities costing up to $15 each. Symbolic Logic: Index. xxxi + 199pp. The Game of Logic: 96pp. 2 vols. bound as one. 5⅜ x 8.
20492-8 Paperbound $2.50

MATHEMATICAL PUZZLES OF SAM LOYD, PART I
selected and edited by M. Gardner
Choice puzzles by the greatest American puzzle creator and innovator. Selected from his famous collection, "Cyclopedia of Puzzles," they retain the unique style and historical flavor of the originals. There are posers based on arithmetic, algebra, probability, game theory, route tracing, topology, counter and sliding block, operations research, geometrical dissection. Includes the famous "14-15" puzzle which was a national craze, and his "Horse of a Different Color" which sold millions of copies. 117 of his most ingenious puzzles in all. 120 line drawings and diagrams. Solutions. Selected references. xx + 167pp. 5⅜ x 8.
20498-7 Paperbound $1.35

STRING FIGURES AND HOW TO MAKE THEM, *Caroline Furness Jayne*
107 string figures plus variations selected from the best primitive and modern examples developed by Navajo, Apache, pygmies of Africa, Eskimo, in Europe, Australia, China, etc. The most readily understandable, easy-to-follow book in English on perennially popular recreation. Crystal-clear exposition; step-by-step diagrams. Everyone from kindergarten children to adults looking for unusual diversion will be endlessly amused. Index. Bibliography. Introduction by A. C. Haddon. 17 full-page plates, 960 illustrations. xxiii + 401pp. 5⅜ x 8½.
20152-X Paperbound $2.25

PAPER FOLDING FOR BEGINNERS, *W. D. Murray and F. J. Rigney*
A delightful introduction to the varied and entertaining Japanese art of origami (paper folding), with a full, crystal-clear text that anticipates every difficulty; over 275 clearly labeled diagrams of all important stages in creation. You get results at each stage, since complex figures are logically developed from simpler ones. 43 different pieces are explained: sailboats, frogs, roosters, etc. 6 photographic plates. 279 diagrams. 95pp. 5⅜ x 8⅜.
20713-7 Paperbound $1.00

CATALOGUE OF DOVER BOOKS

LA BOHEME BY GIACOMO PUCCINI,
translated and introduced by Ellen H. Bleiler
Complete handbook for the operagoer, with everything needed for full enjoyment except the musical score itself. Complete Italian libretto, with new, modern English line-by-line translation—the only libretto printing all repeats; biography of Puccini; the librettists; background to the opera, Murger's La Boheme, etc.; circumstances of composition and performances; plot summary; and pictorial section of 73 illustrations showing Puccini, famous singers and performances, etc. Large clear type for easy reading. 124pp. 5⅜ x 8½.
20404-9 Paperbound $1.25

ANTONIO STRADIVARI: HIS LIFE AND WORK (1644-1737),
W. Henry Hill, Arthur F. Hill, and Alfred E. Hill
Still the only book that really delves into life and art of the incomparable Italian craftsman, maker of the finest musical instruments in the world today The authors, expert violin-makers themselves, discuss Stradivari's ancestry, his construction and finishing techniques, distinguished characteristics of many of his instruments and their locations. Included, too, is story of introduction of his instruments into France, England, first revelation of their supreme merit, and information on his labels, number of instruments made, prices, mystery of ingredients of his varnish, tone of pre-1684 Stradivari violin and changes between 1684 and 1690. An extremely interesting, informative account for all music lovers, from craftsman to concert-goer. Republication of original (1902) edition. New introduction by Sydney Beck, Head of Rare Book and Manuscript Collections, Music Division, New York Public Library. Analytical index by Rembert Wurlitzer. Appendixes. 68 illustrations. 30 full-page plates. 4 in color. xxvi + 315pp. 5⅜ x 8½.
20425-1 Paperbound $2.25

MUSICAL AUTOGRAPHS FROM MONTEVERDI TO HINDEMITH,
Emanuel Winternitz
For beauty, for intrinsic interest, for perspective on the composer's personality, for subtleties of phrasing, shading, emphasis indicated in the autograph but suppressed in the printed score, the mss. of musical composition are fascinating documents which repay close study in many different ways. This 2-volume work reprints facsimiles of mss. by virtually every major composer, and many minor figures—196 examples in all. A full text points out what can be learned from mss., analyzes each sample. Index. Bibliography. 18 figures. 196 plates. Total of 170pp. of text. 7⅞ x 10¾.
21312-9, 21313-7 Two volume set, paperbound $5.00

J. S. BACH,
Albert Schweitzer
One of the few great full-length studies of Bach's life and work, and the study upon which Schweitzer's renown as a musicologist rests. On first appearance (1911), revolutionized Bach performance. The only writer on Bach to be musicologist, performing musician, and student of history, theology and philosophy, Schweitzer contributes particularly full sections on history of German Protestant church music, theories on motivic pictorial representations in vocal music, and practical suggestions for performance. Translated by Ernest Newman. Indexes. 5 illustrations. 650 musical examples. Total of xix + 928pp. 5⅜ x 8½.
21631-4, 21632-2 Two volume set, paperbound $4.50

THE BAD CHILD'S BOOK OF BEASTS, MORE BEASTS FOR WORSE CHILDREN, and A MORAL ALPHABET, *H. Belloc*
Hardly and anthology of humorous verse has appeared in the last 50 years without at least a couple of these famous nonsense verses. But one must see the entire volumes — with all the delightful original illustrations by Sir Basil Blackwood — to appreciate fully Belloc's charming and witty verses that play so subacidly on the platitudes of life and morals that beset his day — and ours. A great humor classic. Three books in one. Total of 157pp. 5⅜ x 8.
20749-8 Paperbound $1.00

THE DEVIL'S DICTIONARY, *Ambrose Bierce*
Sardonic and irreverent barbs puncturing the pomposities and absurdities of American politics, business, religion, literature, and arts, by the country's greatest satirist in the classic tradition. Epigrammatic as Shaw, piercing as Swift, American as Mark Twain, Will Rogers, and Fred Allen, Bierce will always remain the favorite of a small coterie of enthusiasts, and of writers and speakers whom he supplies with "some of the most gorgeous witticisms of the English language" (H. L. Mencken). Over 1000 entries in alphabetical order. 144pp. 5⅜ x 8.
20487-1 Paperbound $1.00

THE COMPLETE NONSENSE OF EDWARD LEAR.
This is the only complete edition of this master of gentle madness available at a popular price. *A Book of Nonsense, Nonsense Songs, More Nonsense Songs and Stories* in their entirety with all the old favorites that have delighted children and adults for years. The Dong With A Luminous Nose, The Jumblies, The Owl and the Pussycat, and hundreds of other bits of wonderful nonsense: 214 limericks, 3 sets of Nonsense Botany, 5 Nonsense Alphabets, 546 drawings by Lear himself, and much more. 320pp. 5⅜ x 8. 20167-8 Paperbound $1.75

THE WIT AND HUMOR OF OSCAR WILDE, *ed. by Alvin Redman*
Wilde at his most brilliant, in 1000 epigrams exposing weaknesses and hypocrisies of "civilized" society. Divided into 49 categories—sin, wealth, women, America, etc.—to aid writers, speakers. Includes excerpts from his trials, books, plays, criticism. Formerly "The Epigrams of Oscar Wilde." Introduction by Vyvyan Holland, Wilde's only living son. Introductory essay by editor. 260pp. 5⅜ x 8.
20602-5 Paperbound $1.50

A CHILD'S PRIMER OF NATURAL HISTORY, *Oliver Herford*
Scarcely an anthology of whimsy and humor has appeared in the last 50 years without a contribution from Oliver Herford. Yet the works from which these examples are drawn have been almost impossible to obtain! Here at last are Herford's improbable definitions of a menagerie of familiar and weird animals, each verse illustrated by the author's own drawings. 24 drawings in 2 colors; 24 additional drawings. vii + 95pp. 6½ x 6. 21647-0 Paperbound $1.00

THE BROWNIES: THEIR BOOK, *Palmer Cox*
The book that made the Brownies a household word. Generations of readers have enjoyed the antics, predicaments and adventures of these jovial sprites, who emerge from the forest at night to play or to come to the aid of a deserving human. Delightful illustrations by the author decorate nearly every page. 24 short verse tales with 266 illustrations. 155pp. 6⅝ x 9¼.
21265-3 Paperbound $1.50

FIVE VOLUME "THEORY OF FUNCTIONS" SET BY KONRAD KNOPP

This five-volume set, prepared by Konrad Knopp, provides a complete and readily followed account of theory of functions. Proofs are given concisely, yet without sacrifice of completeness or rigor. These volumes are used as texts by such universities as M.I.T., University of Chicago, N. Y. City College, and many others. "Excellent introduction . . . remarkably readable, concise, clear, rigorous," *Journal of the American Statistical Association.*

ELEMENTS OF THE THEORY OF FUNCTIONS,
Konrad Knopp
This book provides the student with background for further volumes in this set, or texts on a similar level. Partial contents: foundations, system of complex numbers and the Gaussian plane of numbers, Riemann sphere of numbers, mapping by linear functions, normal forms, the logarithm, the cyclometric functions and binomial series. "Not only for the young student, but also for the student who knows all about what is in it," *Mathematical Journal.* Bibliography. Index. 140pp. 5⅜ x 8.   60154-4 Paperbound $1.50

THEORY OF FUNCTIONS, PART I,
Konrad Knopp
With volume II, this book provides coverage of basic concepts and theorems. Partial contents: numbers and points, functions of a complex variable, integral of a continuous function, Cauchy's integral theorem, Cauchy's integral formulae, series with variable terms, expansion of analytic functions in power series, analytic continuation and complete definition of analytic functions, entire transcendental functions, Laurent expansion, types of singularities. Bibliography. Index. vii + 146pp. 5⅜ x 8.   60156-0 Paperbound $1.50

THEORY OF FUNCTIONS, PART II,
Konrad Knopp
Application and further development of general theory, special topics. Single valued functions. Entire, Weierstrass, Meromorphic functions. Riemann surfaces. Algebraic functions. Analytical configuration, Riemann surface. Bibliography. Index. x + 150pp. 5⅜ x 8.   60157-9 Paperbound $1.50 ·

PROBLEM BOOK IN THE THEORY OF FUNCTIONS, VOLUME 1.
Konrad Knopp
Problems in elementary theory, for use with Knopp's *Theory of Functions,* or any other text, arranged according to increasing difficulty. Fundamental concepts, sequences of numbers and infinite series, complex variable, integral theorems, development in series, conformal mapping. 182 problems. Answers. viii + 126pp. 5⅜ x 8.   60158-7 Paperbound $1.50

PROBLEM BOOK IN THE THEORY OF FUNCTIONS, VOLUME 2,
Konrad Knopp
Advanced theory of functions, to be used either with Knopp's *Theory of Functions,* or any other comparable text. Singularities, entire & meromorphic functions, periodic, analytic, continuation, multiple-valued functions, Riemann surfaces, conformal mapping. Includes a section of additional elementary problems. "The difficult task of selecting from the immense material of the modern theory of functions the problems just within the reach of the beginner is here masterfully accomplished," *Am. Math. Soc.* Answers. 138pp. 5⅜ x 8.   60159-5 Paperbound $1.50

NUMERICAL SOLUTIONS OF DIFFERENTIAL EQUATIONS,
H. Levy & E. A. Baggott
Comprehensive collection of methods for solving ordinary differential equations of first and higher order. All must pass 2 requirements: easy to grasp and practical, more rapid than school methods. Partial contents: graphical integration of differential equations, graphical methods for detailed solution. Numerical solution. Simultaneous equations and equations of 2nd and higher orders. "Should be in the hands of all in research in applied mathematics, teaching," *Nature.* 21 figures. viii + 238pp. 5⅜ x 8. 60168-4 Paperbound $1.85

ELEMENTARY STATISTICS, WITH APPLICATIONS IN MEDICINE AND THE BIOLOGICAL SCIENCES, *F. E. Croxton*
A sound introduction to statistics for anyone in the physical sciences, assuming no prior acquaintance and requiring only a modest knowledge of math. All basic formulas carefully explained and illustrated; all necessary reference tables included. From basic terms and concepts, the study proceeds to frequency distribution, linear, non-linear, and multiple correlation, skewness, kurtosis, etc. A large section deals with reliability and significance of statistical methods. Containing concrete examples from medicine and biology, this book will prove unusually helpful to workers in those fields who increasingly must evaluate, check, and interpret statistics. Formerly titled "Elementary Statistics with Applications in Medicine." 101 charts. 57 tables. 14 appendices. Index. vi + 376pp. 5⅜ x 8. 60506-X Paperbound $2.25

INTRODUCTION TO SYMBOLIC LOGIC,
S. Langer
No special knowledge of math required — probably the clearest book ever written on symbolic logic, suitable for the layman, general scientist, and philosopher. You start with simple symbols and advance to a knowledge of the Boole-Schroeder and Russell-Whitehead systems. Forms, logical structure, classes, the calculus of propositions, logic of the syllogism, etc. are all covered. "One of the clearest and simplest introductions," *Mathematics Gazette.* Second enlarged, revised edition. 368pp. 5⅜ x 8. 60164-1 Paperbound $2.25

A SHORT ACCOUNT OF THE HISTORY OF MATHEMATICS,
W. W. R. Ball
Most readable non-technical history of mathematics treats lives, discoveries of every important figure from Egyptian, Phoenician, mathematicians to late 19th century. Discusses schools of Ionia, Pythagoras, Athens, Cyzicus, Alexandria, Byzantium, systems of numeration; primitive arithmetic; Middle Ages, Renaissance, including Arabs, Bacon, Regiomontanus, Tartaglia, Cardan, Stevinus, Galileo, Kepler; modern mathematics of Descartes, Pascal, Wallis, Huygens, Newton, Leibnitz, d'Alembert, Euler, Lambert, Laplace, Legendre, Gauss, Hermite, Weierstrass, scores more. Index. 25 figures. 546pp. 5⅜ x 8. 20630-0 Paperbound $2.75

INTRODUCTION TO NONLINEAR DIFFERENTIAL AND INTEGRAL EQUATIONS,
Harold T. Davis
Aspects of the problem of nonlinear equations, transformations that lead to equations solvable by classical means, results in special cases, and useful generalizations. Thorough, but easily followed by mathematically sophisticated reader who knows little about non-linear equations. 137 problems for student to solve. xv + 566pp. 5⅜ x 8½. 60971-5 Paperbound $2.75

APPLIED OPTICS AND OPTICAL DESIGN,
A. E. Conrady
With publication of vol. 2, standard work for designers in optics is now complete for first time. Only work of its kind in English; only detailed work for practical designer and self-taught. Requires, for bulk of work, no math above trig. Step-by-step exposition, from fundamental concepts of geometrical, physical optics, to systematic study, design, of almost all types of optical systems. Vol. 1: all ordinary ray-tracing methods; primary aberrations; necessary higher aberration for design of telescopes, low-power microscopes, photographic equipment. Vol. 2: (Completed from author's notes by R. Kingslake, Dir. Optical Design, Eastman Kodak.) Special attention to high-power microscope, anastigmatic photographic objectives. "An indispensable work," *J., Optical Soc. of Amer.* Index. Bibliography. 193 diagrams. 852pp. 6⅛ x 9¼.
60611-2, 60612-0 Two volume set, paperbound $8.00

MECHANICS OF THE GYROSCOPE, THE DYNAMICS OF ROTATION,
R. F. Deimel, Professor of Mechanical Engineering at Stevens Institute of Technology
Elementary general treatment of dynamics of rotation, with special application of gyroscopic phenomena. No knowledge of vectors needed. Velocity of a moving curve, acceleration to a point, general equations of motion, gyroscopic horizon, free gyro, motion of discs, the damped gyro, 103 similar topics. Exercises. 75 figures. 208pp. 5⅜ x 8.
60066-1 Paperbound $1.75

STRENGTH OF MATERIALS,
J. P. Den Hartog
Full, clear treatment of elementary material (tension, torsion, bending, compound stresses, deflection of beams, etc.), plus much advanced material on engineering methods of great practical value: full treatment of the Mohr circle, lucid elementary discussions of the theory of the center of shear and the "Myosotis" method of calculating beam deflections, reinforced concrete, plastic deformations, photoelasticity, etc. In all sections, both general principles and concrete applications are given. Index. 186 figures (160 others in problem section). 350 problems, all with answers. List of formulas. viii + 323pp. 5⅜ x 8.
60755-0 Paperbound $2.50

HYDRAULIC TRANSIENTS,
G. R. Rich
The best text in hydraulics ever printed in English . . . by former Chief Design Engineer for T.V.A. Provides a transition from the basic differential equations of hydraulic transient theory to the arithmetic integration computation required by practicing engineers. Sections cover Water Hammer, Turbine Speed Regulation, Stability of Governing, Water-Hammer Pressures in Pump Discharge Lines, The Differential and Restricted Orifice Surge Tanks, The Normalized Surge Tank Charts of Calame and Gaden, Navigation Locks, Surges in Power Canals—Tidal Harmonics, etc. Revised and enlarged. Author's prefaces. Index. xiv + 409pp. 5⅜ x 8½.
60116-1 Paperbound $2.50

Prices subject to change without notice.

Available at your book dealer or write for free catalogue to Dept. Adsci, Dover Publications, Inc., 180 Varick St., N.Y., N.Y. 10014. Dover publishes more than 150 books each year on science, elementary and advanced mathematics, biology, music, art, literary history, social sciences and other areas.